FLIGHT OF THE MARTLETS
The Golden Age of Sussex Cricket

FLIGHT OF THE MARTLETS
The Golden Age of Sussex Cricket

BRUCE TALBOT AND PAUL WEAVER

Dedication

To Pat, for the love and the laughter. Paul

To Alison, for love and inspiration. Bruce

First published in Great Britain in 2008 by
The Breedon Books Publishing Company Limited
Breedon House, 3 The Parker Centre,
Derby, DE21 4SZ.

This paperback edition published in Great Britain in 2014
by DB Publishing, an imprint of JMD Media Ltd

ISBN: 978-1-78091-427-5

Printed and bound in the UK by Copytech (UK) Ltd Peterborough

Contents

Foreword by Jim Parks

IT TOOK a long time but Sussex got there in the end. The county's first Championship, in 2003, and I was delighted to be the club's president in that year. But success has continued, and now it is three Championships in five years, certainly the county's most successful period ever. And what a great time to write about such success, with last season's memories still fresh in the mind.

The club came close several times over the years: firstly just after the turn of the century, in 1902 and 1903; then in the early 1930s, when the exciting Duleepsinhji was at the fore and the team came second on three successive seasons, 1932 to 1934; next, a year that I remember well, 1953, when the team was led very much from the front by David Sheppard; and later in 1981 under John Barclay.

It seemed that to actually win the title was just a dream until 2003 when, under Chris Adams, and with a well-balanced team, the impossible happened. In the past, Sussex had very good teams but were always just lacking that extra star bowler. In the present set-up this certainly does not apply. The captain has just about everything he wants, and of course he has Mushtaq.

To have that story, and the more intimate details of the Sussex success before you, is quite something, and how nice it would be in five years time if a further sequel to this book could be published, again talking about the current success of the Sussex County Cricket Cricket Club.

Jim Parks

Acknowledgements

IN THE course of our earlier collaboration, *The Longest Journey*, we felt certain that we had exhausted the time and patience of all our many helpers. Clearly, they have gained a second wind in the four years that have elapsed. Either that, or they completely forgot what nuisances we were. As with Peter Falk's Columbo, there was always 'one more thing'.

We would like to thank everyone at Sussex County Cricket Club for their co-operation, but in particular the coach, Mark Robinson, the captain, Chris Adams, and all the players whose recent efforts inspired this book. On the marketing side, Rosalie Birch was a terrific help, while Simon Dyke had more vital statistics than a modelling agency.

Robin Marlar, the club's former captain and chairman, was the source of many interesting and amusing anecdotes – some of which actually related to Sussex County Cricket Club – and he hosted a great lunch to boot. Ian Cameron and Clive Roberts, two of Sussex's biggest supporters, helped get the project off the ground.

We would also like to thank Michelle Grainger and Rachel Beddow at Breedon Books for their unflagging enthusiasm and Simon Dack and James Boardman for providing the superb photographs. Finally, we would like to thank Rob Boddie, the club's venerable librarian, Norman Epps and Jim Pegg for once again fine tooth-combing through the text for mistakes.

Chapter 1
Back to Back

WHO would Sussex be if they were a Premier League football team?

It was not a question you expected to hear in the Sussex Cricketer pub on the evening of 22 September 2007 as Chris Adams and his players got some serious celebrating underway. To be honest, it was difficult hearing anything at all that night above the cacophony of noise created by hundreds of people enjoying themselves, both at the bar and spilled-out into the pub garden. Sussex may be the most successful club in the country at the moment, but they do not have a huge membership (around 4,000 at the start of 2007), and if you are a regular at Hove, as most of the people partying that night were, it is inevitable that the faces of fellow supporters become familiar as you wander around the bleachers at the Sea End or find a deckchair at the Cromwell Road End to watch the cricket.

During that long night of celebration, which followed the longest, most agonising day that any of those supporters had endured, and as champagne was swigged from the trophy as it was passed

The sun sets at Hove, but a long night of celebrations is about to begin for Chris Adams and Sussex after they clinched back-to-back Championships at Hove on 22 September 2007.

Players celebrated back-to-back titles with a parade around the streets of Brighton and Hove.

around the pub, normally quiet, introspective, sober supporters began to lose their inhibitions. The bloke you see sitting in the same deckchair every day as you wander round for an ice cream suddenly decides there is no better time to make your acquaintance properly. That is why I ended up being asked by someone I had seen almost every day during the season, without knowing anything else about him, to compare Sussex to a top-flight football team. Manchester United or Arsenal? Well, the county certainly has a heritage and tradition as long and grand as those two institutions, but I suppose if you had to name two cricket clubs to compare with them it would be Lancashire and Surrey. How about Aston Villa? All I could think of for their equivalent was Warwickshire – occasional moments of inspiration, but living on past reputations for too long. In the end, we settled on Fulham – a small club with masses of tradition, an evocative ground, a loyal fan base, and success, albeit limited, both in the recent and distant past. And usually punching above their weight.

Okay, agreed my new friend. Now imagine if Fulham won three Premier League titles in five years, including two in successive seasons. That would never happen, would it? As a keen soccer fan, Mark Robinson would have appreciated the analogy. Not since the great Essex team of the early 1980s – the side of Gooch, Lever, Hardie, McEwan, Pringle, Foster and Philip – has a county won three titles in five years. Since 1983, only three teams have won successive Championships: Essex again in 1991 and 1992, Warwickshire (1994, 1995) and Surrey (1999, 2000). Winning it once is hard enough but, as Sussex discovered, doing it again the following season is even tougher. This might explain why, in some ways, the celebrations that accompanied the success in 2007 felt even better than those for Sussex's first Championship four years earlier and certainly better than those of 2006, when the title was won under glowering Trent Bridge skies in front of 400 or so Sussex supporters who rattled around in a venue that can hold 40 times that number.

The last Lancashire wicket had fallen at The Oval at 6.04pm to confirm that Sussex would be champions again. But it was another 45 minutes, as the light faded quickly on a glorious late-summer's day, before Chris Adams got his hands on the trophy. The ECB and sponsors Liverpool Victoria had been fretting for most of the afternoon that they would be in the wrong place when the title was decided. They had hedged their bets by waiting at Gatwick for one of the most exciting finales in the history of domestic cricket's blue riband to reach its denouement.

The players' balcony was packed with family, friends and well-wishers, which it had been for most of the afternoon, as everyone anxiously monitored events at The Oval. Adams sneaked away to fulfil his media commitments in the Hove press box, where Christopher Martin-Jenkins, whose final county assignment as correspondent of *The Times* had been the Worcestershire game, had thoughtfully left a bottle of something sparkling in the fridge, just in case. Adams returned to the dressing room as night fell, gathered his players and for a few moments the squad enjoyed some precious time together.

They toasted absent friends such as Luke Wright, who would hear the news of Sussex's triumph in Mumbai airport, en route with the England one-day squad from the Twenty20 World Championships to Sri Lanka. Murray Goodwin, a cornerstone of all three titles, was back in Australia for a family funeral. There was also the painful realisation that this would be the last time this Sussex squad would be together. Rana Naved was heading to Yorkshire, a victim of the ECB's nonsensical decision to reduce the number of overseas players from two to one from 2008 onwards. And then there was Saqlain Mushtaq, whose wish for a move closer to his London home would be granted by Sussex a few days later, even though he still had a year left on his contract.

Just before 8pm, the squad left the dressing room. Around a hundred supporters were still milling around outside to applaud their heroes one last time. Down the access road at the back of the pavilion they went with Adams at the front as usual – a band of brothers for whom the realisation of what they had achieved was starting to sink in. A few moments later they marched into the Sussex Cricketer to a roar that must have been heard on the Hove seafront. Everyone who wanted to touch the trophy, have their picture taken with it or sip champagne from it was able to. Adams, Robinson and the players were determined that as many people as possible would feel part of what had been achieved. They have never lost sight of what makes Sussex cricket unique – the sense of family fostered among everyone involved, from Adams to Mike and Sam the gatemen, from Ruby the scorecard seller to the youngest supporter. You wonder if those unforgettable scenes would ever happen at Old Trafford or The Oval on such an occasion. Probably not.

* * * * *

What is undeniable is that for the past two years the best team have won the Championship. Lancashire supporters will trot out lame theories that if the weather had been kinder to their side the trophy would surely have been back at Old Trafford for the first time since 1934. And there is no doubt that is does rain a lot more in Manchester than it does in Hove. But Lancashire's Mark Chilton, in one of his last acts before resigning the captaincy, acknowledged that Sussex were worthy champions. So did Dale Benkenstein, his Durham counterpart. English cricket's youngest first-class county had gone into the last day of the season top of the table after beating Kent in three days, but they had to settle for second place, 4.5 points behind the champions, despite the crushing nine-wicket win they inflicted on Sussex at the Riverside in the penultimate round of fixtures.

The truth is that, where the Championship is concerned, the best team *always* win. How can it not when the season represents five gruelling months that test each and every participant's physical and mental resolve to its absolute limit? Throw in other factors such as injury, international call-ups and, yes, the weather, and it is no surprise that the players themselves are in total agreement: you do not fluke the Championship. Of all team competitions in English professional sport, it is the toughest to win.

Mark Robinson would have said the same had Lancashire pulled off the most remarkable run-chase in Championship history on the last day, or had things turned out differently in 2006 when the Red Rose county looked favourites until Sussex, inspired by Mushtaq, won three of their last four games.

Mark Robinson and his predecessor Peter Moores view the action at Arundel during Sussex's match with Yorkshire in June 2006.

'Every side can play the bad-luck card,' said Robinson. 'And perhaps that could have been us more than other teams in 2007. We had a lot to deal with – injuries, the Bob Woolmer situation at the start of the season and the fact we had to give up four players to England, which is unheard of for us.

'Over the season the best team comes out on top. How can it not when you play in a competition which lasts five months?'

Had Sussex fallen just short in 2007, Robinson would have been justified in thinking the odds had been stacked too high against his team, although looking for excuses is definitely not his style. In their two previous Championship-winning seasons only three players – James Kirtley, Matt Prior and Mike Yardy – had been away with England and never at the same time. In 2007 they had four England players, with Luke Wright joining the aforementioned trio. Prior only played three Championship matches, and his one appearance after mid-May was on Twenty20 Finals day.

Sussex have prided themselves for years on their ability to keep players fit, but eventually their good fortune with injuries was going to end. At various stages of 2007 they were without Mike Yardy (broken finger), Rana Naved (dislocated shoulder) and Jason Lewry (knee) – all key members of the side. For the title decider against Worcestershire it was a minor miracle that they could field a side, never mind get the victory they required to clinch another title. The county were down to their last 13 players and that included Rageb Aga, the Kenyan-born seamer who had never played a first-class game before. Jason Lewry needed five painkillers a day and two cortisone injections to get through the last three

Matt Prior's glove-work and batting earned him an England Test debut in May 2007, which he celebrated with 100 against West Indies at Lord's.

matches, and talismanic batsman Murray Goodwin was absent too. Wright was with England, Kirtley arrived back from the Twenty20 World Cup in time for the revelry but too late to play against Worcestershire, while Prior was nursing a broken thumb after being hit in the nets by a ball thrown by England coach Peter Moores during the Twenty20 jamboree in South Africa.

Rana's injury was a real sickener. Attempting a typically wholehearted diving stop on the boundary at the Riverside in the penultimate week of the season, he smashed his right shoulder into an advertising board. Play was held up for 35 minutes before he was taken to hospital, where a serious dislocation was diagnosed. It would be five months before he was fully fit again. The sight of him being stretchered off in front of his distressed teammates was not how it was supposed to end for one of the best overseas players in Sussex's history. At the start of the season Rana had been with the Pakistan squad at the World Cup in the West Indies when coach Bob Woolmer collapsed and died the night they were sensationally knocked out of the tournament by Ireland.

The squad and management, including Woolmer's assistant coach Mushtaq Ahmed, were virtually under house arrest for the next few days as Jamaican police attempted to piece together an explanation for Woolmer's death. It hit Mushtaq hard. Nothing seemed to have changed when he returned to

Mushtaq Ahmed asks the question against Kent in April 2007.

England and took 10 wickets as Sussex launched their title defence with a victory over Kent. But he claimed just six wickets in the next three games, and when he tried to escape the media spotlight by spending a few days back home in Lahore he was besieged by reporters investigating the latest crackpot theory surrounding Woolmer's final few hours. It was only in mid-June, when the Jamaican authorities finally concluded that the 58-year-old had died from natural causes, that Mushtaq could get closure on what he described as the worst two months of his career.

'People kept asking me questions here and at home so it was a hard time, but I finally felt relaxed and was relieved when the news came through,' he said. 'Of course there was still a lot of sadness, because Bob was a friend and a great man, and I felt for his family who must still mourn their loss.'

The weather, too, was a factor in a wretched summer – and not just in the North West. Sussex lost the equivalent of 10 full days' play to rain and bad light, including all four of the games at The Oval in the third week of August, their first total washout in four-day cricket. 'The weather was a factor,' remarked Chris Adams, 'but it always is to some degree throughout the season. Last year we were more badly affected than usual, but it is an uncontrollable thing which makes the Championship so hard to win. Until a scientist comes up with a way of not making it rain on cricket grounds between April and September you just have to put up with it – and we did.'

* * * * *

The weather had not been a problem at the start of the season. In fact, April was one of the sunniest and warmest on record, but Sussex had their fair share of problems as they prepared to defend their title. No fewer than five regulars were missing for the annual curtain-raiser against the MCC, a game in which Robinson was hoping to field his strongest side. Mushtaq, who had only arrived 48 hours earlier, decided to work on his fitness in the Lord's nets, while Rana Naved only joined up with the squad once the game was underway. Chris Adams was attending the birth of his third child, Molly; Richard Montgomerie was with his wife, who was having an operation; and, perhaps most worryingly, Jason Lewry had only just begun bowling again after a bacterial infection had laid him low for a fortnight and he had lost a stone in weight.

On the field, there was some comfort for Robinson against a strong MCC side containing five England players. James Kirtley took four first-innings wickets, and when Sussex replied Murray Goodwin and Mike Yardy put together a third-wicket partnership of 225 before Yardy's right index finger was broken by a lifter from Steve Harmison. It was a clean break, but it would keep Yardy out until 30 May and, to compound his frustration, he was on 99 when it happened. Sussex drew the game, and any hopes of a positive outcome were ended by the loss of an hour's play on the final day when a malfunctioning sprinkler sent water trickling down the Lord's slope and onto the pitch, rather than the outfield.

Two days later, Kent arrived for the Championship opener and, with Adams, Montgomerie, Mushtaq, Rana and Lewry restored to the ranks (although Lewry only played because Robin Martin-Jenkins had flu), normal service resumed as Sussex cantered to an eight-wicket win with more than two sessions to spare. The foundations were laid by Montgomerie's 175, his sixth score of more than 150 for the county, in a total of 510 boosted by 62 extras. Mushtaq then took 6–74, including his 1,300th first-class wicket, as Kent subsided to 216. They could only make Sussex bat again thanks to a last-wicket stand of 86 between Min Patel and Robbie Joseph. Sussex needed less than an hour to knock off their target of 56 on the last day.

Adams felt afterwards that his side was still capable of improvement, but it would be another five weeks before supporters witnessed evidence of that. In

Richard Montgomerie was a key member of three Championship-winning teams.

Peter Moores masterminded Sussex's renaissance before joining the England set-up in 2005.

between, they saw two of the poorest Championship performances for years in defeats by Warwickshire and Kent, which drove Robinson to criticise his players in public for the first time since he took over as coach.

On the day his predecessor Peter Moores was being unveiled as the new England supremo, Robinson watched his side produce their by now familiar capitulation at Edgbaston, a venue they have not won at since 1982 and the days of Imran Khan and Garth Le Roux. The pitch was as emerald green as the outfield, and it was only when groundsman Steve Rouse drove the stumps into the ground that the players knew where it was. As is so often the case though, it played easier than it looked. But it was not the first time during the season that Sussex encountered such conditions, designed primarily to negate the threat of Mushtaq.

The leg-spinner still took four wickets, and Rana weighed in with his first five-for of the summer, but Warwickshire's first innings total of 391 was more than competitive. By the end of the second day Sussex, having been rolled over for 151 in 42.5 overs, were following on for the first time in three years. At 111–2 in their second dig they harboured hopes of a fightback, but only Carl Hopkinson, with scores of 47 and 55, showed the necessary gumption and the game was all over before lunch on the third day. Not long after, the players were heading to the practice nets.

Robinson was phlegmatic afterwards and confidently predicted that Sussex would show the mettle of champions at Canterbury. 'There is too much honesty in that dressing room for us not to,' he insisted.

Instead, they produced an even worse performance against Kent as they suffered back-to-back innings defeats for the first time in 10 years. As is often the case, they were undermined by one of their former players. Yasir Arafat scored 122 to lead a Kent recovery from 140–5 to 368 all out, including some masterful stroke-play against Mushtaq, before taking two new-ball wickets. The fragile confidence of the Sussex batsmen was painfully evident on day two. On another seamer-friendly surface even experienced players like Goodwin and Adams struggled and by mid-afternoon, after scores of 102 and 160, they were heading home. For once Mushtaq was subdued against the county he has taken more wickets against (93) than any other.

The inquest continued over the next couple of days. 'All of a sudden we were being written off after three games, which was a surprise in some ways, but not so if you had seen those two performances,' admitted Adams.

'Our batsmen struggled on two similar pitches, and I was perhaps guilty of over-bowling Rana and Mushtaq, especially at Canterbury, although Jason Lewry got injured after only bowling a few overs. It was a tough couple of days, but we seem to have those sorts of wobbles every season. I suppose we were fortunate in a way that we had ours fairly early on, when we knew there was lots of time to improve.'

There were no green shoots of recovery in evidence a fortnight later, when Surrey visited Hove and dominated for the first three days. By the end of the game, however, the champions had definitely re-discovered some of their self-belief, thanks to an outstanding rearguard action led by Murray Goodwin. It was going to take something special to upstage Mark Ramprakash. The best batsman in England scored 266 not out as Surrey made 626–3 declared, the highest team total at Hove since 2002. He put on 403 with Mark Butcher – the biggest third-wicket partnership against Sussex in Championship history and the second-highest stand for any wicket by any team at Hove. Goodwin held the reply together with his 50th first-class hundred, but that was only by way of a warm-up for the 34-year-old. When Sussex began the final day they were still 226 behind with eight second-innings wickets in hand, and a third successive defeat loomed despite the placid nature of the pitch.

But Goodwin batted through the day to finish on 205 not out – the sixth double hundred of his Sussex career and the second time he had scored two centuries in the same match for the county. It was familiar territory for Goodwin. A year earlier he had produced a similar performance to save the game against Warwickshire, and as well as the personal milestones it helped his side get the season back on track.

'We analysed those two defeats, but it was important to keep the dressing room a positive place, and I'm glad saving that game helped us do that,' said Goodwin. 'It was a pivotal moment in our season.'

Adams also scored a hundred, while Richard Montgomerie and Chris Nash made good runs. Suddenly, Sussex had a few batsmen in form, and when they travelled to Worcester a few days later they also had a full-strength bowling attack, with Lewry fit enough to replace Kirtley. The game followed a familiar pattern for the sizeable contingent of Sussex supporters who needed little excuse to crow 'That's why we're champions' from the back of the Basil D'Oliveira Stand. Adams won a crucial toss and his side rattled up 512. Goodwin made his third successive century and Carl Hopkinson fell 17 runs short of his maiden Championship ton.

Mushtaq then took 5–22 as Worcestershire were skittled for 100 in just over a session and although Graeme Hick's 134th first-class century held Sussex up on day three victory was wrapped up just before tea. A few moments later it was raining heavily and did so throughout what would have been the fourth day. Even the weather gods were smiling on Sussex again.

'The talk at the start of that game was to win it in three days,' recalled Robinson. 'That wasn't arrogance because you have to earn the right to say that, but I loved it when we talked about how we were going to win. We played ultra-aggressive cricket, and it was great to watch.'

Sussex were still 22 points behind early pacesetters Yorkshire as they prepared to face Lancashire at Hove, but there had been a discernible shift in their mood. A bullish Adams put the visitors in after a frustrating first-day washout, but Stuart Law scored his sixth hundred against Sussex and no one could pass 50 in the champions' reply.

When Lancashire declared on the final day, they set Sussex a target of 303 in 66 overs and an early finish looked likely when Montgomerie and Nash quietly put on 93 for the first wicket. But Muttiah Muralitharan took his match haul to nine wickets with four more victims, and it needed a gutsy innings from Andrew Hodd to secure the draw.

'It was three days of very intense cricket played at the highest level,' reflected Adams. 'It was hard but fair and probably ended with the right result.'

Already the table had a congested look, with just 27 points between Yorkshire, rejuvenated under Darren Gough, at the top, and seventh-placed Lancashire, but to keep hopes alive of another title Sussex needed at least one win from their two fixtures before the three-week hiatus for the Twenty20 Cup.

Shane Warne's Hampshire held the advantage when they reduced Sussex to 233–8 on the first day at Arundel on 6 June, but Luke Wright and Mushtaq both made perky half-centuries as the last two wickets added 108 runs. The momentum had shifted, and Sussex pressed home their advantage in the manner of champions. Mushtaq took 7–72, the best figures by a Sussex bowler at the Castle Ground, and his side built on their lead of 139 thanks to 103 from their captain. Goodwin was out for 99 for the second time in his Sussex career before the declaration left Hampshire 500 to win. Everyone expected another Mushtaq masterclass, but the key incisions were made by Wright and Martin-Jenkins, who took five wickets between them

Robin Martin-Jenkins, a key member of all three title-winning teams, has lift-off against the Indian tourists at Hove in July 2007.

as Sussex wrapped up victory by 166 runs with more than a session to spare on the final day. There is no love lost between Adams and Shane Warne and their exchanges in the middle were as competitive as ever. But the Hampshire captain had the good grace afterwards to admit that his side were outplayed once Sussex's tail had wagged so vigorously on the first day.

Sussex were now second, just five points behind Yorkshire, but their first meeting of the season at Headingley was a soggy anti-climax. The outfield was under water for much of day one and it was a miracle that play started when it did after lunch on the second day. Damp, muggy conditions were ideal for swing and seam, but after bowling out the leaders for 139 Sussex could only muster 141 in reply, despite being 52–1 at one stage. Yorkshire declared at tea on the final day and set Sussex a notional target of 283, although the stalemate was confirmed after just 22 overs, the match ending in farce as Younis Khan and Jacques Rudolph bowled five overs in eight minutes off one-pace run-ups in an attempt to avoid a fine for a slow over rate.

Wins for Hampshire and Lancashire meant the top five were separated by just 12 points going into the Twenty20 break, but Adams and Robinson were confident that their side was back on track.

'I was proud of the way we had recovered from those two bad defeats early on, although the response the players produced did not surprise me,' said Robinson. 'We have done it before, and I knew there was the strength of character in our dressing room to do it again.'

Championship action resumed on 13 July and Sussex went to the top of the table for the first time. Durham were rolled over by an innings and 102 runs before lunch on the third day at Horsham, with

Spectators enjoy the sunshine and a big Sussex win against Durham at Horsham in July 2007.

More success for Mushtaq Ahmed, this time against Durham at Horsham in July 2007.

some familiar foes overpowering the visitors, who had only beaten Sussex once in the Championship. Mushtaq finished with nine wickets in the match, including his 50th of the season, and the seamers all chipped in, but the highlight was Adams's superb 193, which delighted a big Saturday crowd at Cricketfield Road. Chris Nash and Andrew Hodd, who was still bubbling after scoring his maiden first-class hundred against India the previous week, both made half-centuries on their home ground as Sussex built a lead of 308 before dismissing Durham for 206 in their second innings.

Afterwards, Adams predicted that three more wins from their seven remaining games would be enough to secure the title. How prophetic those words turned out to be. What he perhaps could not have dared hope was that the first of them would be achieved a fortnight later against their main rivals Lancashire at Liverpool, where Sussex had been making unsuccessful visits for 100 years.

Before they headed north, the county had drawn a rain-ruined contest against Hampshire at the Rose Bowl. At midday on the first day, with the temperature just 14 degrees and the floodlights piercing a slate-grey sky, it felt more like mid-April than high summer. In the circumstances, Adams's decision to bat first on a damp pitch was a big surprise. What was less of a shock was that they soon slumped to 64–6. The captain was scathing about Hampshire's decision to allow the use of artificial light in Championship games (something Sussex do not do at Hove) and was in bullish mood again when the umpires decided to restart the game on the third afternoon. In his opinion, the damp outfield was not

Rana Naved celebrates a wicket against Durham at Horsham in July 2007.

fit for play, and Wright tore a groin as he slipped when making a stop and was ruled out for the next 10 days. Only 135 overs were possible, and the game ended in a draw.

At least the sun was shining when Sussex arrived on Merseyside to encounter another pitch that was never going to last four days. Lancashire were boosted by the return of Andrew Flintoff, who was giving his injured ankle a run-out, and with 13 internationals in action this was a heavyweight battle in every sense of the word.

The game did not disappoint. Sussex slumped from 221–4 to 274 all out despite excellent half-centuries by Goodwin and Nash, but they managed to restrict Lancashire's lead to 27, with Stuart Law falling five runs short of another hundred against his favourite county attack. Sussex lost both openers before they had wiped out their arrears, and by tea on the second day 22 wickets had fallen. But, in one of the most compelling sessions of the season, Goodwin and Mike Yardy withstood a fired-up Lancashire attack to put Sussex back in the match, and although they both fell quickly on the third morning, useful runs down the order from Adams and Carl Hopkinson, returning to the side in place of Wright, left Lancashire with a target of 242 and the best part of five sessions to score the runs.

At 65–1 they were cruising when Adams came up with the defining moment of the match – and probably of the season itself – a stunning catch low to his left at second slip to remove Law. 'It was the best catch of my career,' was the skipper's proud boast afterwards, and no one who witnessed it was inclined to disagree.

Lancashire capitulated in the face of hostile seam bowling by Martin-Jenkins, Rana and the indefatigable Mushtaq, who finished with six wickets. Out of respect to their opponents, Sussex did not treat Lancashire or the stunned Aigburth crowd to a rendition of *Sussex by the Sea*, but both sides were only too aware of the significance of the result. It was Sussex's first win at Liverpool in 16 attempts.

'I knew we could take the title again after we won that game,' reflected Adams. 'I have never played a county game of such intensity. The umpires said it was like a Test match and I agree. It was fantastic to come out on top.'

Sussex now had a lead, albeit a slender three points, at the top, but it did not last long. They returned to Hove full of confidence and on another slow turner felt confident enough to give Saqlain Mushtaq his debut in a two-pronged spin attack against Warwickshire. Between them, Saqlain and Mushtaq took 16 wickets, but Sussex batted abysmally in their first innings when they were dismissed for 168 after their top order was dismantled by the gentle away swing of Adam Shantry, who took the first four wickets.

Warwickshire declined to enforce the follow-on, despite a lead of 265, as insurance against batting last on a wearing pitch. They eventually set Sussex 504 to win, and there were periods on the last day when the county looked capable of achieving what would have been the highest fourth-innings chase in Championship history. Montgomerie's magnificent 195 was the cornerstone, and he thoroughly deserved a maiden double hundred. But when Goodwin and Adams fell in quick succession after lunch, the run-rate dropped and Sussex had to settle for a draw.

Frustratingly, Sussex lost their place at the top of the table without bowling a ball in anger. All four days of the match at The Oval against Surrey in the third week of August were abandoned – the county's first complete washout since the advent of four-day cricket. Meanwhile, up at Scarborough, the only washouts were relegation-bound Warwickshire, who were beaten with a day to spare by Yorkshire to set up a tussle between the top two at Hove on 5 September.

The visitors included Michael Vaughan, Inzamam-ul-Haq and Matthew Hoggard in a powerful line-up, but they had no answer to a fired-up Sussex, whose victory by an innings and 261 runs was their biggest in the Championship since 1923.

'If you get 11 good individual performances, as there were in that game, you are going to get a decent team display as well,' reflected Adams after one of the best Sussex displays under his command. Perhaps it was the pre-match incentive offered by academy batsman Michael Gould that inspired Sussex. He said he would have his head shaved if Sussex won in three days and the cheers of an appreciative crowd outside had barely died down when Jason Lewry reached for the clippers to induct another skinhead into the dressing room.

Adams had won the toss, and Sussex made the most of it by piling on a massive 597–8. Mike Yardy rediscovered his form with the first hundred of a frustrating season, and it was followed by a maiden Championship century from Hodd as Sussex's last three wickets added 187 to demoralise the visitors. What followed was all too predictable. Mushtaq completed another five-for, including the prized scalp of his great friend Inzy, but if the many disgruntled Yorkshire members thought their side's first innings had spoiled their holiday, they were incandescent with rage after an even feebler second-innings display, which saw them bowled out for just 89. Rana Naved finished things off with three wickets in five balls to take his season's tally to 50, while Mushtaq bowled only one over.

Sussex now had a five-point lead over Yorkshire and a game in hand, with Hampshire and Lancashire a further nine points behind. There was even the possibility, albeit a remote one, that a hefty victory at

Mike Yardy on his way to a century against Yorkshire in August 2007.

the Riverside in their penultimate game, combined with results elsewhere, could secure the title with a game to spare. But, this being Sussex, no one seriously thought they would do things the easy way.

The county had never lost at the Riverside and despite the absence of Prior, Wright and Kirtley – who had linked up with England's Twenty20 World Championship squad – they were confident of extending that fine record. Adams took first use of another grassy pitch, but his side were outgunned by Durham's heavy seam attack. Martin-Jenkins made an unbeaten 77 – his highest score of the season so far – and Goodwin a more prosaic 66, while quite a few umpiring decisions did not go Sussex's way. But 291 was an inadequate first-innings score and when Durham, fortified by a maiden hundred from opener Mark Stoneman, reached 247–3 in reply, things looked bleak. However, the terrible injury suffered by Rana Naved, just after lunch on the second day, seemed to inspire Sussex rather than demoralise them. Saqlain and Mushtaq shared seven wickets as Durham collapsed and their first-innings lead was just 25. But Sussex were soon in trouble again at 27–3 and when Adams, who top-scored with 44, departed early on day three it was a case of *when* Durham would win rather than *if*. They knocked off their target of 107 for the loss of just one wicket.

As Sussex headed back down the A1, their hopes of retaining the title were fading. Lancashire had thrashed Warwickshire to go six points clear and Sussex were struggling desperately with injuries and availability. As well as Rana, they would be without their World Cup trio and Goodwin, while Saqlain and Mushtaq were suffering with knee problems. Even Adams had a badly bruised foot.

'Bearing in mind all that had happened during the season, we did well to still be in contention going into the last game,' admitted the captain before heading south.

Sussex were fortunate that their final opponents were a Worcestershire side already relegated. Even before Adams won the toss, the most likely scenario was that Sussex would need Surrey, who were at home to Lancashire, to do them a favour. Durham, away to a demob-happy Kent side who had staved

Mushtaq Ahmed in action against Worcestershire in September 2007, when he took 13 wickets as Sussex clinched their

Chris Liddle appeals unsuccessfully against Worcestershire in the title-clincher at Hove in September 2007.

off the threat of relegation, were waiting for any slip-ups by the top two.

For the second successive home game Sussex scored more than 500 in their first innings, although no one reached three figures. The top four all passed 50, with Nash and Montgomerie putting on 155 in their last opening stand together. Martin-Jenkins ended the season with a flourish, but he fell one short of what would have been his first hundred since 2003.

Mushtaq then got to work. Six wickets in the first innings meant that Worcestershire followed-on 319 behind, and although they showed more fortitude second time around

Richard Montgomerie has some special memories of his last day as a professional after collecting his third Championship-winners' medal at Hove in September 2007.

they were only delaying the inevitable. On the final morning Sussex took the remaining five wickets, with Mushtaq having claimed seven more to take his tally for the season to 90. It made him the leading domestic wicket-taker for the fifth successive year. A crowd of around 3,000 stood in warm appreciation, first for the retiring Montgomerie, who led the players off, and then for 'Mushy', who was so tired he could barely raise an arm to acknowledge the cheers. It was 12.20pm – but Sussex would not be confirmed champions for nearly six hours.

Surrey had dominated Lancashire for the first three days, thanks to the imperious Mark Ramprakash, who scored a hundred in each innings. They eventually set Lancashire 489 to win, but it was not until Dominic Cork inside-edged off-spinner Murtaza Hussain with Lancashire just 25 runs short of victory that the celebrations could begin.

'Awful' and 'excruciating' were perhaps not the words you would have expected Adams to use to describe a third Championship in five years, but they were a succinct summary of that surreal Saturday afternoon at Hove as everyone waited for Sussex's fate to be decided 50 miles up the A23. The players had pointedly ignored live TV coverage of the Surrey game for the first three days. Now, when they were desperate to watch it, the television sets in the ground could not receive Sky's interactive broadcast. Matt Prior even rushed home to see if his Sky card would do the trick, but to no avail.

Hove, September 2007, and the party is underway.

Online radio coverage was hit-and-miss, so all Adams and his men could do was monitor events via Teletext, text messages from mates or the reaction of the hundreds of supporters who had stayed on in anticipation of another celebration.

'Waiting around was just dreadful – one of the worst experiences of my career,' said Adams. 'We were just waiting for the crowd to react.'

Lancashire kept going for it – they had no choice – and all the time that arch-competitor Dominic Cork was at the crease they still had hope. But shortly after 6pm the County Ground erupted. Seconds later, the players' balcony was awash with champagne, and the first rousing rendition of *Sussex by the Sea* was being sung by a crowd of several thousand overcome by a mixture of elation and relief.

The party begins at Hove in September 2007.

So what chance a hat-trick? Well, the good news is that if Sussex do successfully defend their title the celebrations will again take place on home turf, with Yorkshire due at Hove for the last match of the season. If nothing else, the revelry is always so much better when it takes place in front of your own supporters.

* * * * *

Not that the players seemed to mind too much at Trent Bridge, on that rainy September afternoon in 2006, when they cavorted in front of the 400 or so fans from Sussex, most of whom had journeyed to Nottinghamshire that morning in anticipation of a celebration, after clinching their second Championship. While the three Pakistanis in the squad – Yasir Arafat joined the party on the day he signed for Kent for 2007 – toasted the victory with nothing stronger than diet cola, Adams was dementedly spraying champagne from the dressing-room balcony before joining the Sussex fans shoehorned into the Trent Bridge pavilion, where the trophy was passed around and the barman, who was expecting to knock off early, had to call in more beer.

So was 2007 better than 2006? Coach Mark Robinson concedes that last year's victory was harder to achieve because of all the obstacles Sussex had to overcome, in particular injuries and England call-

The only disappointment in the success of 2006 was that only 400 or so Sussex fans were at Trent Bridge to witness it.

Title number two is celebrated at Trent Bridge in September 2006.

ups. He said 'History will tell you how hard it is to win two in a row, but as to whether it was better than 2006 I think I will only be able to answer that question in a few years because I see our back-to-back Championships as part of an era of success for Sussex, not the end of it.'

History will also judge that Sussex played better cricket on a more consistent basis in 2006 than they did the following season. Their start – six wins in the first eight games – was exceptional, and they finished with three wins in the last four matches. Adams also won the toss 10 times.

Lancashire were familiar and persistent foes and must have felt sure that the pennant would finally be fluttering over Old Trafford when they routed Sussex in two days at Liverpool and hung on for the draw at Hove in August with their last two batsmen at the crease. But while Sussex finished strongly, Lancashire drew their last six games.

'After the start we had, we knew, whatever happened, that we were going to be there or thereabouts at the end,' recalled Adams. 'Lancashire pushed us all the way, but I don't think anyone could deny that we were worthy champions.' Sussex clinched the title on 22 September – the latest date in a season it had been won for 28 years.

Richard Montgomerie, who scored seven fifties but only converted one of them into a century, thought 2006 was more like Sussex's first Championship in 2003 than the one which followed it. It was good for their waistlines as well, he reckoned. All cricketers love their food, but Montgomerie remembers countless lunchtimes during the season when the players happily left sponge pudding and custard on the dining-room table. He said 'When that bell rang we couldn't wait to get back onto the field, we were down the stairs and ready. We had been the same in 2003 – it was a good sign.'

Robinson had a dream start to his first season as coach. In the first two months Sussex won 10 of the 12 games they played as they quickly set the pace in the Championship and won all five of their matches in the C&G Trophy – a momentum that was to take them all the way to their first Lord's Final since 1993.

The Championship opener against Warwickshire ended in a draw, but Murray Goodwin had put himself in the record books again. His stand of 385 in the second innings with Mike Yardy, which helped to save the game, was the second-highest for any wicket by the county. Yardy made 159, while Goodwin lodged an unbeaten 214 as Sussex negotiated the final day without losing a wicket, after being outplayed for most of the first three. The Zimbabwean scored another double hundred later in the season, but this was to be his personal highlight. 'I wanted to average more than 60 (he finished with 1,649 runs at 63.42), and that innings set the tone,' he said.

Conditions at Hove had been ideal for batsmen seeking early-season form. In contrast, every run was a precious commodity at the Rose Bowl a week later when only Robin Martin-Jenkins made a half-century against Hampshire on a wicket that started damp and was condemned by Robinson and Adams, even though their side eventually won a remarkable game by 94 runs.

In his first appearance of the season Rana Naved took five wickets to help Sussex take a lead of 44, while Martin-Jenkins's 91 – his highest score for two years – set Hampshire a target of 306. They were nicely placed at 144–3 when they were unravelled by a familiar scourge. Mushtaq Ahmed had vowed to improve his record in early-season games. It can be hard for the little man to feel magic in his fingers when his hands are permanently cold and pitches, such as this, are unresponsive. His hands spent most of this match buried deep in his pockets, but he still finished with 7–64, five of his victims being given out leg-before by former Hampshire player Trevor Jesty.

More success for Rana Naved.

Murray Goodwin scores another boundary against Yorkshire at Arundel in June 2006.

The momentum was maintained a fortnight later at Headingley, where Rana Naved relished showing Yorkshire the error of their ways. He had been on trial there a few years earlier during a stint in the Bradford League, but Yorkshire did not pursue their interest despite the promptings of former England captain Ray Illingworth. A match haul of 11–148, the best by a Sussex bowler in Yorkshire since 1907, took Rana's tally to 71 wickets in 11 games since arriving halfway through the 2005 season. Carl Hopkinson, looking more confident in his new opener's role with every match, impressed Darren Lehmann with his unflustered approach, while Matt Prior made a first-innings century and then guided his side to a five-wicket win with an unbeaten 55 on the final day. Prior rated his 12th hundred as the best of his career because of the maturity he showed, especially when he added 49 for the last wicket with Jason Lewry to secure an unexpected third batting bonus point.

Amazingly, after two wins and a draw, Sussex were only third in the First Division table, behind two clubs with similar records, Lancashire and Warwickshire. 'I'd have put my mortgage on us being top at that stage,' said Adams. 'It just showed what a great League it was shaping up to be again.'

Champions Nottinghamshire arrived at Hove a few days later and promptly bowled out Sussex for 143, their lowest total in two years. But Mushtaq led a fight-back with six wickets after a bizarre incident when he was confronted by Chris Read on the boundary's edge moments after Mushtaq had dismissed the wicketkeeper for a duck. Read later apologised and the matter was settled at the end of play with a handshake in the umpires' room. Hopkinson held Sussex's second innings together with a patient 74 – his highest score of the season – but their last five wickets tumbled for 13 runs to leave Notts with a straightforward target of 161, and at 49–1 they were cruising.

Bowlers around the country had noticed that the 2006 Duke balls were swinging more. Here, Rana and Lewry also got it to reverse-swing after just 20 overs, aided by a square which was unusually dry and abrasive for such an early stage in the season. They took seven wickets between them. Mushtaq chipped in with the other three and Sussex won by 40 runs. Now they were top of the table.

Sussex had achieved three successive wins – all inside the distance – but there was even better to come at the Riverside in the third week in May when Durham were routed in five sessions, with all but one of their wickets falling to Sussex's brilliant Pakistani duo. Mushtaq's match haul of 10–37 included a burst of 5–10 in 4.1 overs, as shell-shocked Durham collapsed from 47–0 to 80 all out in their second innings. What was even more surprising was that, in an age when preparing for an individual opponent has never been easier thanks to the technology available, Durham coach Martyn Moxon admitted his side had been unable to find any footage of Mushtaq to view.

Despite making only 229 themselves, Sussex still won by an innings. Typically, Mark Robinson also chose to highlight the contribution of Robin Martin-Jenkins, whose 49 was crucial in the context of a low-scoring contest and maintained his early-season form with the bat. 'And of course they all love Mushy and Rana,' said Robinson. 'They earned everyone two extra days off!'

Sussex headed to Horsham with a 21-point lead, where they reeled off a fifth successive win, this time against struggling Middlesex. Only Owais Shah, who has consistently played Mushtaq better than anyone else in recent seasons, scored a stylish hundred on a pitch where his teammates found Mushtaq almost unplayable. The leg-spinner finished with 10 wickets, but the festival highlight was Jason Lewry's

stunning diving catch at mid-on to remove Shah in Middlesex's second innings, when they began their forlorn pursuit of a target of 490. Like Adams's effort at Liverpool in 2007, it was a seminal moment in the 2006 summer.

Mushtaq's influence extended off the field too as the search for a replacement for Rana began. On his recommendation, Sussex signed Yasir Arafat, hitherto known only to supporters for his stints in Scotland's Pro40 League team while he was professional with Clydesdale CC in Glasgow. Arafat linked up with his new teammates for the first time at Horsham. 'He does not have much

Yasir Arafat proved an excellent short-term overseas signing in 2006.

As well as his captaincy and batting talents, Chris Adams is an outstanding slip fielder. Here he celebrates with Jason Lewry after removing Lancashire's Mark Chilton at Hove in May 2007.

of a reputation now, but he will have by the end of the season,' predicted Mushtaq. He was not wrong.

With five wins out of six and a 23-point lead at the top Sussex headed to Liverpool for a summit meeting with Lancashire at the beginning of June in a fantastic position, but the strain was beginning to show. They had played virtually non-stop throughout May and the day after beating Middlesex had lost their first one-day game of the season. Rana was missing after hurting his knee at Horsham, an injury which was to keep him out for the first two months of Pakistan's tour of England. Even so, it was still a surprise to see Sussex bullied into a two-day defeat by a Lancashire seam attack that relished a bouncy, grassy Aigburth pitch. The only consolation was a 500th first-class wicket for Lewry, which was warmly acknowledged by the Liverpool crowd on the second morning. 'We had not really had a proper break since the season started, and against Lancashire we looked very jaded,' admitted Adams. 'Lancashire outplayed us, but they still knew that we would be a threat to them for the rest of the season.'

In the next eight days Sussex played just once – a routine C&G victory in Ireland – and when they returned against Yorkshire at Arundel in mid-June they looked refreshed and revitalised. Arafat made an encouraging Championship debut with bat and ball. His 86 really rubbed Yorkshire's noses in it after Murray Goodwin's magnificent 235 and a first hundred of the season from the captain had helped Sussex take a lead of 312, which justified Adams's unusual decision to bowl first at home. Australian Darren Lehmann scored a sublime 130 in Yorkshire's second innings, while Arafat took three wickets, including England captain Michael Vaughan in what turned out to be his last appearance of the season before another appointment with the knee surgeon. 'That was one of our most satisfying victories of the season,' recalled Mark Robinson. 'Everyone was expecting a positive reaction after the Lancashire defeat and we delivered. It is very rare that we play badly for two games in a row.'

England captain Michael Vaughan, playing for Yorkshire, has his stumps rearranged by Jason Lewry at Arundel in June 2006.

Lancashire reeled off three successive wins to open up a six-point lead, and when the Championship programme resumed three weeks later, after Sussex had failed to qualify for the knockout stages of the Twenty20 Cup, a familiar face was absent. For the first time since he joined Sussex, Mushtaq Ahmed missed a four-day game, because of a neck injury. It was to trouble him for several weeks and although he returned for the next match against Middlesex it was obvious he was still suffering. The country was enjoying one of its hottest summers for years and a fully-fit Mushtaq would have relished the dry conditions. But in three games in high summer he took a modest 12 wickets, five of them in one innings against Warwickshire, which made his achievement in the last four fixtures, when he took 37, even more remarkable.

Batsmen dominated when Kent visited Hove on 13 July. Mike Yardy, Murray Goodwin and Matt Prior all made hundreds, and although some supporters thought Adams over-cautious in delaying his declaration for 30 minutes on the final day he knew Kent were capable of chasing big targets. Off-spinner Ollie Rayner took three wickets on his Championship debut and Arafat struck with successive deliveries, but Matt Walker kept Sussex at bay with an unbeaten 70 after twice being dropped.

It was even warmer at Southgate a few days later before the first rain for weeks denied Sussex what would have been a certain victory on the final afternoon. Another slow, flat pitch was

Matt Prior playing a typically attacking stroke against Nottinghamshire in June 2005.

desperately hard work for the bowlers, including the returning Mushtaq, and the game was heading for stalemate when the captains evoked the days of three-day cricket by coming up with a last-day target for Middlesex of 421 by means of contrivance. The chief beneficiary of this was Murray Goodwin, whose unbeaten 156, which contained 19 fours and 11 sixes, came off 45 balls in 50 minutes of joke bowling. Middlesex had their last two batsmen at the crease as they clung on for the draw between the interruptions in the final session.

Ollie Rayner appeals against Sri Lanka at Hove in May 2006. The all-rounder scored a hundred on his first-class debut in this match.

With Lancashire losing at Kent, despite the presence of Andrew Flintoff, the title race was as open as ever, but Sussex's next destination was Edgbaston, a place guaranteed to bring them out in a cold sweat. This time they should have improved on their dismal record there, but chasing 267 on a wearing pitch they were bowled out for 256 after Montgomerie and Yardy seemed to have done the hard work with a second-wicket stand of 138. Sussex had been bowled out in one session in their first innings before Mushtaq, back to something like his old self, had set up the chance of a first win in Birmingham for 24 years with 5–39 in Warwickshire's second innings. Matt Prior, suffering from a hamstring strain, was replaced by Andrew Hodd for Warwickshire's second innings. It was a setback, and Sussex were entitled to think that events were conspiring against them a few days later when they had the opposition's last two batsmen at the crease for the second time in three games but were unable to force a victory.

This time it was Lancashire's Mal Loye, who batted for much of the final day, and number 11 Gary Keedy who kept them at bay. They survived the last eight balls of a contest every bit as good as its pre-match billing, which attracted record gate receipts for a Championship game at Hove, with crowds of around 3,000 each day. Sussex had dominated thanks to hundreds from Prior, Richard Montgomerie and Mike Yardy, and although Stuart Law got his customary century against Sussex, Lancashire were always on the back foot. What did not help Sussex was another injury to Mushtaq, who suffered a groin strain and could barely hobble up to the crease on the last day when he was expected to win the game. The county did go back to the top of the table, but their lead over Lancashire was just a single point, and their rivals did have a game in hand. Loye's joyous reaction at the end was indicative of the relief in the visitors' dressing room at not conceding the advantage to their main rivals.

By the time they returned to action against Durham 11 days later, Sussex had lost their lead after Lancashire picked up 12 points from a drawn Roses match. But the break had clearly done them good. Mushtaq had briefly returned to Pakistan to attend the birth of his fourth child and came back rejuvenated. A pinched nerve in his neck was still troubling him, but regular visits to the massage table had eased his discomfort and his rehabilitation continued when he took eight wickets as Sussex won by an innings and 133 runs with five sessions to spare. Chris Adams had earlier made a season's best of 155, while up at Old Trafford Lancashire picked up 11 points from a soggy draw against Middlesex. The teams were level on points with three games to go. Lancashire had two home fixtures to Sussex's one, but while they were back on track Lancashire suddenly appeared incapable of forcing precious victories.

Rain frustrated both sides in their next matches. Sussex had the better of things at home to Hampshire at the beginning of September, when Goodwin lodged his seventh hundred of the season and Chris Nash made 67 after replacing Mike Yardy, who was with England's one-day squad. Only 38 overs were possible on the third day, which ended any hopes of a positive outcome, while a last-day washout at Blackpool frustrated Lancashire when they were well placed to defeat Warwickshire. The sides were now level on points with two games to go, but Sussex were on top after winning more matches. They had the chance to open up a gap when their rivals missed the next round of fixtures. They took it, too,

Murray Goodwin celebrates another century.

but only after one of the most fraught run chases in Sussex's history had earned them a two-wicket win over Kent at Canterbury.

Sussex managed to eke out a precious first-innings lead of 48, despite some nervy batting, and Mushtaq strengthened their position with another outstanding display. He took 6–58 in Kent's first innings and trumped that performance with 7–74 in the second, taking him to 89 wickets for the season. Arguably, though, Mushtaq made an even more important contribution with the bat on an unbearably tense third day. Chasing 161, Sussex slumped to 145–8, but with James Kirtley at his obdurate best at the other end, Mushtaq scored the best 13 not out of his career. When the winning runs came shortly after 3pm the roar of relief in Sussex voices, both in the dressing room and among the many supporters, could be heard at Old Trafford.

'That game was real pressure,' said Adams. 'I didn't sleep much the night before the third day, which is a sure sign that it's going to be tense. Unless you experience it you can't really put into words how hard it is to win a game like that when a wicket falls every eight overs. I think we all knew after winning at Canterbury that the title was ours to lose.'

Sussex had opened up a 19-point lead, and Lancashire needed to win their game in hand against relegation-threatened Durham in the penultimate round of fixtures. But after a second-day washout at Old Trafford took the total number of overs they had lost to 1,000 (compared to Sussex's 175), their chances receded. All of which made it even more puzzling that Glen Chapple and Dominic Cork came off 11 overs early on the third day because of low sun at the Stretford End. Lancashire picked up 11 points, which left Sussex with an eight-point advantage as they headed to Trent Bridge for the final game. Lancashire were at the Rose Bowl, where Hampshire's slim hopes of leapfrogging the top two ended when Sussex picked up their first bonus point at Trent Bridge.

Sussex's build-up was not ideal. Three days earlier they had thrown away the chance of a domestic treble when they lost to Nottinghamshire in the Pro40 League, which gave Essex the title even though they were also beaten in their final game. Sussex refused a request from England to rest Yardy ahead of the Champions Trophy, while Rana returned after recovering from his knee injury

Mike Yardy is particularly fluent on the leg-side.

with some encouraging performances in the one-day series against England for Pakistan.

Adams won the toss, but nerves seemed to play a part again when Carl Hopkinson was run out for a duck. Sussex recovered thanks to Yardy's eighth Championship century in two years. Hove will always be where the heart is for the left-hander, but after a successful England debut there a few weeks earlier Yardy was clearly enjoying Trent Bridge as well. Sussex had achieved their first objective of maximum batting points by the end of the first day, despite losing Goodwin for 99 in the final over. Adams was confident. 'I knew at lunchtime on the first day that we would win,' he said.

Matt Prior and Robin Martin-Jenkins punished some wayward bowling on the second morning before Adams declared on 560–5 at lunch. Six players had passed 50 in a Sussex innings for the first time since 1904. Significantly, Nottinghamshire now needed to get the single batting bonus point they required to retain their First Division status. Either that or win the game. In the event they did neither. The growing contingent of Sussex supporters in the Fox Stand was starting to get a little twitchy when Nottinghamshire reached 143–3 in reply, especially as Lancashire were getting on top at the Rose Bowl, but they need not have worried. Sussex took four wickets in 13 balls, two of them by Martin-Jenkins, as Notts slumped to 144–7 before being bowled out for 165. By the close they had subsided to 50–4 following-on, all of the wickets falling to Mushtaq, who now had 97 for the season.

Sussex's only worry now was the weather. The only guarantee the forecasters could offer for day three was that it would rain at some stage, although the appearance of TV weatherman John Kettley in the press box the following morning was perhaps a sign that all would be well. Mushtaq's big moment came when Ryan Sidebottom had an ugly swipe across the line and saw his off-stump flattened. For the second time in four years, Mushtaq had taken 100 Championship wickets. He sank to his knees, kissed the turf and, in his mind at least, offered a simple prayer of thanks. His teammates stood respectfully for a couple of seconds before submerging him with congratulatory hugs.

Thirty minutes later he had taken 9–48, the best figures of his career, and the best by any bowler at

Mushtaq Ahmed in full cry.

Trent Bridge since 1936. In his last two games Mushtaq had taken 26 wickets. No one had done more to drag Sussex over the finishing line once again. They finished 18 points clear at the top, six fewer than in 2003 but considerably more than their winning margin in 2007 of just 4.5 points.

* * * * *

It was full five hours after the trophy presentation before the last Sussex player left the dressing room to continue the celebrations at the team hotel, while supporters reluctantly began dragging themselves back down the M1. Seven of the side who had clinched Sussex's first Championship in 2003 had done it again – Adams, Goodwin, Mushtaq, Prior, Kirtley, Lewry and Martin-Jenkins – and for their captain the overwhelming emotion was relief.

'It had been tough and much harder than 2003, even though that went to the last game as well. At the end of June I thought we would win it comfortably, but the second half of the season was a real grind, with Lancashire pushing us all the way. With four games to go I told the boys we needed three wins and they delivered them.'

Kirtley might have felt like the villain of the piece for denying Mushtaq all 10 wickets in Nottinghamshire's second innings, but this triumph meant more on a personal level than 2003. A year

Jason Lewry celebrates.

earlier his career was in jeopardy after he was forced to re-model his action again. Now, in the space of a few weeks, he had been Man of the Match in a Lord's Final and helped Sussex win their second title.

Martin-Jenkins had flourished under Robinson, too. 'A great man-manager as well as a great coach,' he admitted, while Jason Lewry had his best season since 1998 with 52 wickets, enough to earn him another contract. But it was the performances of the younger players which convinced Adams that Sussex were establishing a legacy that would last long into the future. Luke Wright, Carl Hopkinson, Chris Nash, Ollie Rayner and Andrew Hodd all played significant parts in 2006 and were to be even more prominent a year later.

'Each Championship has been special for different reasons,' said Adams. 'But for me the best thing about 2006 was that we were pretty consistent all season. Even when we didn't win for four games, we still had the opposition nine wickets down twice and eight down against Kent, so I knew we were still in good shape.

'We had the best bowler in the country in Mushtaq and the best batsman in Murray, but time after time someone stepped forward to set up a game for us, and it wasn't always one of our star performers. We had some of the best individual performers in the country – but we also had the best team.'

As Adams continued his celebrations in the Trent Bridge dressing room his place in Sussex's history was already assured. Now, after winning the domestic double, he could rightly claim to be their best-ever captain, too. Yet within a few weeks Adams had decided to leave the county, only to have a dramatic change of heart. If Trent Bridge had been another massive high, the weeks which followed were to be the most turbulent of his career.

Luke Wright's terrific county form earned him England recognition in 2007.

Chapter 2
Grizzly – Yorkshire and Back

IT IS the bottom of the fixture list, rather than the top, which Chris Adams always looks at first when the new season's schedule is unveiled. It carried even greater significance in 2008, with Adams hoping to become the first captain since Yorkshire's Brian Close 40 years ago to win three Championships in a row. With that in mind, and considering how Adams could easily have been leading the opposition rather than Sussex, he could not help but smile when he saw that Sussex's last game this season is against Yorkshire. 'At least it's at home,' he said. 'And if we do make it a hat-trick let's hope we don't have to wait six hours to start celebrating!'

Adams's place in Sussex history has long since been secured. Leading the county to the first Championship in their history in 2003 did that. Now he must be regarded as their best skipper of all time, having led Sussex to two more titles, as well as their first one-day trophy for 20 years, two promotions in the one-day League and a place at the Twenty20 Finals for the first time.

'I'm fulfilled,' he said, once the dust had settled on Championship number three. 'I have achieved more than I could ever have hoped to on a personal level. If I could have one wish it would be that I could carry on being captain of Sussex forever. But my time will come to an end soon and then I will be happy to wind down and finish my career under a different captain.'

As memories of that remarkable September afternoon in 2007 started to fade, Adams signed a contract extension which tied him to the club until the end of the 2009 season, when he will be 39. There

Happy and content, the Sussex captain, Chris Adams, reflects on an unprecedented era of success for the county under his leadership.

was never any doubt, provided he still had the appetite for the job, that 2008 would be his 11th season as captain, the eight-year county record of Arthur Gilligan set in the 1920s having long since been surpassed.

Who knows whether Adams will complete 13 years in charge. As he prepares for the new season he is not even sure himself. Were he to lead Sussex to a hat-trick of Championships, he might feel there could be no better way to finish. Were Sussex to fall short, then he could think it the right time to hand over to a younger man, almost certainly his vice-captain Mike Yardy, whose personal stock rose during the winter with his intelligent leadership of the England Lions team. Adams has no doubt about the worthiness of his successor, even if it will probably be the end of the 2008 season before he decides whether to hand over or not. 'Michael will be a leader more than worthy of the honour and trying to continue our success in the future.'

And what next? Adams would love to finish a career, which began 20 years ago, with 50 first-class hundreds and 100 fifties to his name. He started 2008 with 48 and 91 respectively, so that personal ambition looks certain to be fulfilled, barring serious injury. But Adams has had his eye on the bigger picture for some time now.

'I am the stage of my career when I look beyond playing and have been for some time now,' he said. 'I would love to stay in the game in a director of cricket or managerial role, and when the right job comes along I would put my name to it. If that position is with Sussex then perfect – that is the ideal scenario.'

As soon as Peter Moores got the call from his country to become the ECB's academy director in 2005 Adams made it clear that he fancied being his replacement as Sussex's director of cricket. His lack of experience – particularly in coaching – counted against him, although he has since undertaken the ECB's level-four coaching course. When the chief executive's job at Hove became vacant in 2006 Adams was interviewed and impressed the panel. But Gus Mackay got the job, presumably because of his hands-on experience in helping to turn around struggling Leicestershire, allied with his cricketing background as a former Zimbabwe international.

Adams's staunchest ally at Hove remains chairman David Green, who has been in charge for much of the Adams era. 'David is one of the most honourable men I have ever come across and in all my dealings with him he has always acted with the utmost integrity,' said Adams.

Green would love nothing better than to give Adams a long-term role, but a county such as Sussex is not in a position financially to simply invent a job for him. With Mackay and coach Mark Robinson likely to be *in situ* for some time to come, Adams will continue to look elsewhere for the opening into management he has set his sights on, which is why it cannot be said with 100 per cent certainty that he will still be a Sussex player when his current contract expires. Early in 2008 he was interviewed for both the newly created full and part-time roles within the England selection set-up. Someone of his experience of the county game looked tailor-made for at least the part-time role, which would also have enabled him to carry on playing for Sussex, but once again he was overlooked.

Peter Moores and Chris Adams celebrate after Sussex won the Second Division of the Totesport League in 2005. It was Moores's last day as Sussex coach.

Chris Adams ponders his options.

Perhaps the ties that bind him to Sussex cannot be broken now. The closest Adams has come to leaving was in October 2006 when it seemed certain he would join Yorkshire in the dual role of captain and director of cricket, only to change his mind almost at the same time as he was being unveiled at a press conference at Headingley and pictured in a Yorkshire shirt. It was the biggest crisis in Sussex cricket since the 'revolution' of 1997, which paved the way for the era of success under Adams. Had the offer come from another county Adams would probably have not been tempted. But he was born just a couple of miles across the Yorkshire border in north Derbyshire, and when he decided to leave Derbyshire in 1997 he would have joined Yorkshire had they made him an offer, even one less lucrative than that which eventually lured him to the south coast.

Yorkshire's first approach had been made at the Professional Cricketers' Association dinner, three days after the Championship had been won at Trent Bridge in 2006. 'It's always a top night because all the players go and it's a great place to do a bit of detective work, to find out which players are available,' recalled Adams. 'Official approaches are not allowed until 31 October, but tapping-up goes on all the time, particularly at that dinner. It was where we first got wind that Tony Cottey might be unhappy at Glamorgan and interested in coming to us back in 1999.'

Now it was Adams's turn. 'I didn't know who Stewart Regan (Yorkshire's chief executive) was until he introduced himself. He said he had spoken to (Yorkshire coach) David Byas and that my name had come up as someone who might restructure their cricket operation. I gave him my mobile number and that was it, the conversation cannot have lasted more than a minute.'

Regan called the following day and arranged to meet Adams in London four days later with Yorkshire chairman Colin Graves. Things were moving fast. 'For the next 48 hours I thought of little else,' said Adams. 'But I knew at some stage I would have to front-up with Sussex. I cannot remember how many times I tried to call David Green and held back. When I finally spoke to him it was outside a fish and chip shop in Hassocks of all places, funnily enough somewhere David had recommended to me.

'He was shocked, as I knew he would be, but gave me his blessing to talk to Yorkshire. I should have been pleased but I felt deflated. I'd got it into my head that Sussex were happy for me to leave when, as I was to discover, it was nothing of the sort.'

Adams met Yorkshire's top brass the following day. 'Like Regan, I didn't know Colin Graves from Adam, but he obviously knew Adams. After 10 minutes of small talk he suddenly said "Down to business!" and the small talk was over!'

Yorkshire's vision, which had been outlined to their board by Geoffrey Boycott, was a scenario where Adams would call the shots on and off the pitch. 'Captaining Yorkshire was not going to swing it for me, but the director of cricket job did appeal. I gave them my own ideas and explained that by bringing in key personnel I thought I could get the structure right. The more we spoke, the more I warmed to the idea, and the financial package was mind-blowing.

'When I told David Green the next day his first question was: "How can you turn it down?" I reiterated that if Sussex put a three-year contract in front of me on the same terms I was on at the time I would sign it there and then, but David was in an impossible situation. Had it been up to him alone I think he would have, but he had the committee to consider and the best the club could offer was a year's extension, with the option of another year after that.'

During a coaching course at Loughborough the following week, Adams had dinner with Peter Moores and dropped his little bombshell. 'Pete told me the offer was too good to turn down. My wife Sam and the kids were settled in Sussex and we had just moved house so it would be a massive wrench but by then my mind was made up.

'I emailed David just to make sure everything was agreed. His sign-off line was "Everything which glistens isn't necessarily gold." They proved to be prophetic words, but a few minutes later, and a fortnight after I had first met him, I rang Colin Graves to accept the job.'

A meeting in Yorkshire was arranged, and the following day, while Adams was being unveiled to the media, his family were shown around houses in the Leeds area. His mind seemed to be made up, but by the end of that day he was having his first serious misgivings.

'We drove to Leeds on a thoroughly miserable day weather-wise, made worse by hold-ups on the M1. It took an age to get through Leeds because of the rush-hour traffic, and I will never forget looking into the rear-view mirror and seeing my two girls' faces. They were as miserable as the weather. Sam was still being very supportive, but I could tell that Georgia and Sophie were deeply unhappy at the upheaval which lay ahead.'

Adams's worries increased after he met Graves and Regan again. Michael Lumb had left to join Hampshire and Anthony McGrath still wanted to leave. And Yorkshire's insistence that Adams would have full control over player recruitment was starting to sound like an empty promise when Regan announced that he had just signed Pakistan's Younis Khan for the 2007 season.

'I was stunned,' said Adams. 'I really started to have my doubts then, but it felt like I was on a conveyor belt and couldn't get off. The next day, before the press conference, we went through my restructuring proposals. I wanted a first-team coach and physiologist and David Byas's new role as head of cricket development clearly defined. But my plan to bring in two new people was dismissed out of hand.

'I was expected to say how proud I was to be at Yorkshire when 10 minutes earlier they had poured scorn on my plans for restructuring. I fronted up as best I could and I still genuinely felt then that we could compromise and sort everything out.'

More meetings followed the following week, one of which was with the players. 'That went well. I had already spoken to (England captain and Yorkshire player) Michael Vaughan, who was very positive, and I tried to convey a sense that this was the start of a new adventure for them as much as me. I think they all left in a positive frame of mind, but the same could not be said of me.

'That night I cannot have slept for more than 30 minutes. I knew there would be some serious battles to be fought, and for the first time I realised that in batsman, captain and manager perhaps I had bitten off more than I could chew. I'd done two of them well at Sussex but three? What about my relationship with Regan and, having met the players, did I honestly think they could become my team?

'By 5am I was wide awake and felt physically sick. All I wanted to do was be with my wife and kids, and by 9 o'clock that morning I was, having driven straight back down the motorway. As soon as I walked through the door Sam knew something was up. I told her I couldn't go through with it.'

Later that day, news broke which was even more of a shock to Sussex supporters than Adams's departure two weeks earlier. He was staying. Within an hour of returning home he was at David Green's house and then he drove to the ground. 'When I asked Mark Robinson if I could stay, he hugged me and told me it was the best news he'd had for ages. You can't imagine how relieved I was when he said that.' By mid-afternoon Adams had signed Sussex's original contract offer.

The only issue remaining was the call to Regan. 'Naturally, he was stunned and insisted I meet him and Colin Graves to see if a deal could be salvaged. No contract had been signed and I said I would be happy to talk to Graves, but I didn't want to meet him face-to-face. That phone call never came.'

Eighteen months on and Adams has no regrets. 'It was the hardest decision I have ever made in my career, but it was the right one at the time and still is. I had underestimated how big a job it was and I wonder whether I would have been too much for Stewart Regan. But I still admire him. He works 24/7 to better Yorkshire cricket. Unfortunately, when it came down to it I couldn't offer the same level of commitment.

'People compared what happened to when Peter Moores left, but the big difference was I was going to be playing for another county and pulling on a different shirt, and I just did not feel as inspired about that as I should have done. They say never let your heart rule your head. But throughout it all my heart completely turned my head around.'

With the whole affair conducted in the public eye, other counties were alerted to the fact that Adams was, and still is, happy to speak to any county that feels they have something on offer. In

August 2007, in the week before he led Sussex in the Twenty20 Finals for the first time, he was approached by his former club, Derbyshire, about becoming club coach. TV presenter Nick Owen, who in 2008 was the public face of a successful takeover of his beloved Luton Town FC, is Derbyshire president and a close friend of Adams. He made an unofficial approach, but it went no further than that and a few days later, after denial and counter-denial about whether he had been approached, the job went to Adams's former teammate John Morris.

Adams has fought some battles at Hove during his time, but it would have been hard for even his sternest critic to imagine a successful Sussex side without him at the helm. No one, least of all the man himself, pretends that Adams has the people skills of a Mike Brearley or the tactical acumen of a Ray Illingworth or Brian Close. But he is a natural captain, someone who commands respect by leading from the front. England batsman Andrew Strauss has played against Adams several times during his Middlesex career. 'You know you are in a battle with Chris as soon as you toss up,' he said. 'He is one of the most competitive captains on the circuit.'

* * * * *

Adams has also been one of the most destructive English batsmen of the last 20 years, so it seems somewhat ironic when he says that one of his earliest cricketing memories was being taught to bat by imagining that he was rocking his teddy bear to sleep. There were many influential figures in his formative years, not least his father John, who was playing cricket in the sloping back garden of their home in Whitwell on the Derbyshire-Yorkshire border with his other son, David, when Lyn Adams gave birth to Christopher John at home on 6 May 1970.

'Football and cricket were my main loves and still are,' recalled John. 'The boys developed their passion for the game in the back garden and playing for Staveley Miners Welfare CC. I remember when Chris got his first hundred for the Under-13s – I realised then that he could play the game and that he had a level head on his shoulders.'

But the person who most influenced the young Chris Adams was Benita White, who ran coaching sessions for the Cricket Lovers' Society in Chesterfield and first encountered Adams as an eight-year-old. 'She was a fantastic lady, and it was through her that the whole thing started. My father decided that David and I needed proper coaching, saw an advert in the local paper, and took us along. Benita took us under her wing. "Right," she said, "We're going to make cricketers of you."'

And the teddy bear comparison? 'When you are kids you remember things like that' said Adams. 'If you visualise how you hold your bat, you've got your arms in a round with your elbows sticking out and when you're batting the action that you do is rock your bat backwards and forwards, as if you're rocking your teddy bear to sleep.'

It was one the proudest moments of Benita's life when the stocky kid she had first encountered more than 20 years earlier made his England Test debut in South Africa in 1999. She died aged 71 in 2004, and Adams and another of Benita's protégés, Somerset and former England all-rounder Ian Blackwell, were among the many mourners.

John Adams was also one of the Football Association's regional coaches in the north and encouraged Chris's other love for football. It nearly led to his sporting career taking a different path. 'I was at Chesterfield Grammar School and decided when I was 16 that I would leave after completing my O-levels and take up a YTS option. I was a centre-half and had three offers from Chesterfield, Barnsley and Scunthorpe. Sheffield Wednesday also offered me a month's trial.'

It was then that Mike Stone, who ran the Derbyshire Cricket Association, took a hand in Adams's career. He told the lad's parents that he could complete his A-levels at Repton School on a sports scholarship. Adams broke Richard Hutton's run-scoring record in his first year there, but did not complete his second. In 1987 he was offered his first professional contract for three years by Derbyshire.

He made his Championship debut against a Surrey attack led by the fearsome West Indian Sylvester Clarke at The Oval in June 1988. The following season he established himself in the Derbyshire side, playing in seven Championship games and scoring 79 against a strong Lancashire attack of Wasim Akram, Phil DeFreitas, Ian Austin and Mike Watkinson – all international players. Four years after first representing his country as a spinning all-rounder in England Schools Under-15s, he played for England Under-19s, where his colleagues included a certain Dominic Cork. For the next two decades the pair would be teammates and then fierce rivals. By 1990 Adams was a regular in the Derbyshire side and two years later he was awarded his county cap. That season he topped 1,000 runs for the first time with 1,109 at 41.07. He was happy playing for the county of his birth and envisaged a long career there. The England selectors were also starting to take notice of his clean hitting and exceptional ability as a close catcher.

Then things started to unravel in the Derbyshire dressing room. Two of Adams's close pals, John Morris and Peter Bowler, left in 1995, the year after Adams had signed a new five-year contract. Derbyshire's decision to persist in preparing green, seamer-friendly pitches frustrated Adams, who felt the wickets should have been more helpful for their batsmen. 'I scored 1,742 runs that season, so no one could accuse me of not knuckling down, but we were not getting the best out of the team. We had this fantastic array of seamers whom we would have backed to bowl well on any pitch, but we weren't scoring enough runs as a side.

'I told the club that it was fine if that was their policy, but if it was the case, would they let me go elsewhere, where I would have the chance of consistently scoring the volume of runs and forcing myself into the England reckoning. An A tour would have done – I just wanted to make the next rung on the ladder. Derbyshire's reaction was one of bitterness, and I spent the next two years fighting a losing battle with the county's establishment while my career went nowhere.'

The arrival in 1996 of Australians Dean Jones and Les Stillman as the county's new captain and coach enthused Adams again, and Derbyshire finished second in the Championship. But tensions in the dressing room soon re-surfaced. 'I was warned at the end of 1996 to be very careful what I said in there because some of the guys could not handle what we were telling them,' Jones remembers.

The county imploded in 1997, with some players aligning themselves behind Jones and Stillman – including Adams and England bowler Devon Malcolm – while others wanted Kim Barnett, the most successful skipper in their history, to resume the captaincy. Halfway through the season Jones abruptly resigned and headed back to Australia, leaving Stillman with few allies, except Adams, in a dressing room, where the atmosphere was becoming more and more poisonous. Jones left with a parting shot at some of the senior players and Adams was completely out on a limb. When Sussex arrived at Derby for a game in June of that year they were astonished to see one of the best slip-catchers in the country banished, like some naughty schoolboy, to fielding third man at both ends.

Les Stillman sympathised with Adams. 'Chris blossomed under Dean. I came with that Australian attitude of "one in, all in", where you put your hat on your head and that means you're a mate of the other 10 wearing it too. Chris brought into that, but the Derby dressing room had a lot of unstable people obsessed with contracts and their careers.' Like Adams, Stillman found himself ostracised and told to take the second team to a game in Kent. Stillman never coached again, while Adams finally got his wish to leave after threatening to take Derbyshire to court, sparking off a scramble for his signature involving nine counties. Two days before Derbyshire met Sussex in a NatWest Trophy quarter-final in August 1997, Adams met Sussex's new chief executive Tony Pigott at a service station on the M1.

'I went there thinking there was no way I was going to sign for a bottom-of-the-table side like Sussex, but in half an hour Tony sold the club to me and a month after signing my contract I was offered the captaincy because Peter Moores was going to step up and become our coach.'

In 1998, the most successful captain-and-coach partnership in Sussex's history was born. The improvement on the pitch was immediate, as Sussex rose from bottom to seventh place. Adams averaged 42.92 and finally earned England recognition when he played in two one-day internationals against South Africa. The following year he scored more than 2,000 runs in all cricket and earned a place in Duncan Fletcher's first England squad for the tour to South Africa.

For Adams it was the best of times and worst of times. Fletcher backed him by playing him in all five Tests, but he scored just 104 runs in his seven innings at an average of 13.

In the final Test at Centurion, which was to gain notoriety for South African captain Hansie Cronje's infamous declaration, Adams walked out to bat to be greeted by these immortal words from wicketkeeper Mark Boucher: 'Mr Adams, welcome to the last day of your Test career.'

'How right he was,' remembers Adams. 'I got one run that day and, as far as Test cricket was concerned, I knew that was probably it for me.'

Adams may not have been good enough for the supreme test, but given his consistent record over the years it is remarkable that he played only five one-day internationals. He maintains that the intransigent attitude of the selectors in the limited-over series which followed the Tests cost him a long career in international one-day cricket.

In the second match in Cape Town, Adams made 42 – his highest score – and should have seen England to victory. But he holed out coming down the pitch to try and slog Lance Klusener over the top, and England lost by one run. His critics, who felt Adams was still too impetuous in his shot selection, had a field day. In the next game he made just a single as England were routed by a Zimbabwe side inspired by Henry Olonga, who took 6–19. It was to be Adams's last taste of international cricket and the start of one of the worst weeks of his life.

'We flew to Kimberley for the next game when [captain] Nasser Hussain wandered over after we'd done our warm-ups: "Sorry mate, we've decided to give Darren Maddy a go in this one."

'It took a while to sink in, and the other lads were sympathetic. I had to stop Darren Gough from going to Fletcher to find out why I had been dropped. I was depressed, but determined to remain the model pro. Finally, four days later in East London, I followed Nasser to his hotel room seeking an explanation. He told me that the word from back home was it was time to look at Maddy. By "back home" I assumed he meant [chairman of selectors] David Graveney. He said that the way I got out in Cape Town had no bearing on the decision and promised I would play again in the series.'

Instead, a few days later Adams flew home wondering whether he would ever see his daughter Sophie alive again.

'She'd had three epileptic fits in 24 hours. One is quite common, two is worrying and three is very

worrying. The doctor told me to get back as soon as possible. The worst-case scenario was that Sophie might not pull through. I got the next flight out of Johannesburg, and the following morning I was driving from Heathrow to home fearing the worst.'

Thankfully, Sophie recovered and while it was good to spend time with his family again, Adams felt duty-bound to return to the tour: 'I phoned Graveney and said I felt it important to go back, as there were still three more matches in the series. As far as I was concerned it was unfinished business. He seemed sympathetic, but the message came through that I was better off staying at home, but they would call me if any of the batsmen got injured. In other words, they had made their minds up about me.'

Chris Adams in action against Surrey at Horsham in June 2000.

Adams struggled to recover from the realisation that his England career was effectively over at 29. Two much-publicised rows the following summer, first with Essex's Danny Law and then the umpire David Constant, led to rebukes and fines from the authorities and his county: 'I was very aggressive. I wanted to fight the world that season.'

The Law incident was blown out of all proportion. Adams pushed the former Sussex player, but neither umpire saw the incident. Law would have settled for an apology over a pint at the end of play, but his captain, Nasser Hussain, sent in a three-page report and Adams was carpeted by the ECB. Things did not go to plan on the field either. Sussex finished bottom of the Championship in 2000, and Moores and Adams needed the staunch support of the then chairman Don Trangmar to ride out the storm when others felt it was time for a change.

'The supporters were fed up because we had gone from top to bottom in six weeks, but a year later we showed everyone we could go the other way when we won promotion.'

In 2001 Sussex won nine games, two more than any of their rivals, to gain a place in Division One, which they consolidated a year later after overcoming a traumatic pre-season during which

Chris Adams and Peter Moores with Sussex's first Championship trophy in 2003.

A proud Chris Adams was surrounded by past and present Sussex players who gathered in 2004 to celebrate the county's first Championship in their long history.

Spoils of victory. Hove, September 2003.

We are the champions. Chris Adams celebrates on the Hove balcony in September 2003.

Umer Rashid drowned on the club's tour of Grenada. And then there was 2003 and the start of an unprecedented era of success in Sussex's history.

If his career were to end today, Chris Adams would be fulfilled. He has represented his country and been at the helm during the greatest few years in the history of county cricket's oldest club. Molly became the latest addition to the Adams family when she was born just before the start of the 2007 season, and earlier this year the family moved from Hurstpierpoint to a new house near Albourne. 'This is our sixth home since

Chris Adams is flanked by James Kirtley and Sean Heather amid a shower of champagne after lifting the C&G Trophy at Lord's in August 2006.

Chris Adams shows off the C&G Trophy during the parade to celebrate Sussex's twin triumphs in 2006.

Chris Adams celebrates a second Championship.

we moved to Sussex, but I think we will be here for a long time,' he said.

But as he prepares for his 11th season in charge, Adams admits that the extent of what he and Sussex have achieved in the last five years has still not properly sunk in: 'And I doubt if it will until I have long since retired and I'm telling my grandchildren all about my life in cricket.

'All three Championships have been different. I have to say that I will always regard the first one in 2003 as the pinnacle of my career because of the magnitude of what we had achieved in the context of the long history of the club. And also because so many of our supporters were there to see it.

'2006 engendered a feeling of relief more than anything else. It was a gruelling campaign physically, because we were trying to be successful on two fronts. Fortunately, we managed to win the C&G Trophy Final at Lord's in August and the momentum of that day carried us over the finishing line in the Championship. By the time we got to Trent Bridge, we were simply glad to get the job done.

'And then there was last year. Despite what some of our critics would have you believe, we did play some good cricket at times. How important was that magnificent victory over Lancashire at Liverpool in August? And what about the performances in the last two home games against Yorkshire and Worcestershire – games we simply had to win? They weren't bad either.

'At times we were hanging on just to survive – the Warwickshire and Surrey games at Hove spring to mind – and at the start of the season, when we lost successive matches by an innings, we had to show real fortitude and courage. It is testament to the character of the squad that we recovered as well as we did.

'You don't fluke the Championship. It is a fiendishly difficult competition to win because it tests you in so many ways, both mentally and physically. The best side always wins though – and I am proud to say that it was us in 2007.

'I enjoyed last year as much as any other because the contest with Lancashire and all the others was so competitive – which is something I thrive on. Standing toe-to-toe with the opposition and not backing down is what I am all about and what this team is all about.'

Who knows? Perhaps Adams's long-term future may lie away from Hove. The overtures from Yorkshire and Derbyshire have braced his many admirers in Sussex to expect the worst. But this observer, who has followed his Sussex career closer than anyone, believes there are still a few more chapters to come.

Chapter 3
Mushtaq Ahmed: the Greatest Ever?

MUSHTAQ AHMED, it might be argued, is the greatest overseas signing in the history of county cricket. There can be no definitive answer to this rainy-day taproom question. It is not something that can be measured in runs and wickets alone. Certainly the influence Mike Procter had at Gloucestershire extended beyond his heroically fast bowling and powerful batting in the late middle-order; he was the very essence of the side. Garry Sobers's performances for Nottinghamshire – like Procter and many others, he arrived in 1968 – merely underlined what most people had already suspected: here was the greatest all-round cricketer the game had ever seen.

There are some who bracket Malcolm Marshall with Dennis Lillee as the greatest of fast bowlers. Here was a deeply intelligent bowler, not just a thrillingly fast one, a player who could swing the ball both ways at great speed and, to the delight of his captain, bowl and bowl until the ball was ripped from

All seems happy in Mushtaq Ahmed's world.

his grasp. At Lancashire, Clive Lloyd's fielding was as inspiring as his languidly powerful batting, and much the same could be said about Viv Richards at Somerset.

One-day trophies were seized, but not one of these great cricketers succeeded in winning the ultimate prize for his county. At Sussex, the oldest county and, essentially, a small one, the great prize of the County Championship had never been held aloft. Mushtaq was the principal reason why Sussex won not one Championship but three in the space of five years. And for that reason alone he should rank at least alongside the more celebrated names mentioned above. He not only bowled his side to victory after victory, but he made those around him believe in themselves. He helped develop a team ethic in what can often be a selfish game. He played a leading role, in 2003, in a fundamental shift in the dressing-room mindset, that success, and failure, was now down to the team and not one or two isolated individuals.

The impact on Sussex County Cricket Club made by Mushtaq is immense and will never be forgotten. But if your recall ever falters – and this could be associated with acute short-term memory loss, so consult a doctor – take a drive to the Rose Bowl. It is about an hour from Hove, driving westwards along the M27, through Arundel and Chichester and the hundred or so roundabouts that separate them. This is Hampshire chairman Rod Bransgrove's Camelot, where fantasy and glass fibre have come together to produce an attractive new cricket facility, just off the motorway, east of Southampton.

There was an ambition to play international cricket here, and soon Test cricket will be played there too. But the main aim was to win the County Championship for the first time since 1973. In this, Bransgrove has been unsuccessful, though the county came second in 2005 and third in 2006. To bring the title to the Rose Bowl, Hampshire hired the considerable services of Shane Warne. Some say that Warne is the best bowler of them all, ahead of the fast men and medium-pacers as well as his fellow twirlers. Others claim that he is simply the finest spin bowler of all time. Another still more conservative bunch are content to describe him as the greatest leg-spinner there has ever been, and here the dissenters are few. Richie Benaud, no slouch himself, places him ahead of the two great contemporary Australians, Bill O'Reilly and Clarrie Grimmett. But while Warne has struggled and failed to bring the Championship to Hampshire, Mushtaq Ahmed has been the main reason why Sussex have won a fistful of titles over the same period. It is worth engaging with Hampshire supporters in an effort to solve this conundrum. It is not that they can explain it – because they can't – but they can get very cross and bewildered as they try to, which is great fun.

While Warne would have sauntered into a World XI of any era, or even the all-time World XI we regularly choose to play Mars, Mushtaq has struggled to regain his Test place in the Pakistan side in recent years. But, season in and season out, the little miracle from Sahiwal has consistently outperformed one of the game's great legends. Warne's appearances, of course, have been more fitful since he first played for Hampshire in 2000. In 2005 Australia staked a prior claim, but when he has played a full season he has still come second best to the bearded, chuckling, bouncy Mushtaq, who has been the most successful bowler in county cricket for each of the past five summers.

The magician, Mushtaq Ahmed.

Mushtaq took 103 Championship wickets in 2003, 84 in 2004, 80 in 2005, 102 in 2006 and 90 in 2007, giving him a total of 459 wickets at 24.69. That is an average of nearly 92 wickets a season. Warne, too, has had five seasons of county cricket – 2000 and four from 2004. And he has taken 276 wickets for Hampshire at 25.58. In his four full, or full-ish, years of 2000 (70 wickets), 2004 (51), 2006 (58) and 2007 (50) he was not in Mushtaq's class as a consistent winner of matches. Warne has taken five wickets in an innings on 18 occasions for Hampshire, with one return of 10 in the match. Mushtaq has 39 five-fors and 15 match ten-fors.

Even when they go head-to-head, Warne sometimes struggles to keep up. At Arundel last June, when Sussex won by 166 runs, Warne had figures of 5–91 in the first innings. Mushtaq responded with seven for 72 and had a couple in the second innings too, when Warne failed to take a wicket. How can this be explained? Shaun Udal plays for Middlesex now, but he was Warne's vice-captain at Hampshire and met Sussex many times in recent seasons.

Udal said: 'What Mushy has achieved at Hove has been extraordinary. He had been a very decent bowler at Somerset in the Nineties. But when he joined Sussex in 2003 I didn't see him as the missing link that would turn a good side into a Championship-winning one. And yet that is exactly what he became.

'But there is a history of spinners getting wiser and better as they get older, and that's certainly been the case with him.

'From the point of view of the batsman, there is just no getting away from him. He's always at you and there are very few free balls.

'Most of his wickets are bowled or lbw. Generally, he doesn't look to take the ball away from the right-hander in the classical way of leg-spinners. That is what Shane tends to do, getting batsmen caught behind nicking big leg-breaks. Mushy bowls lots of googlies and ones that go straight on.

'Most wrist-spinners like a bit of bounce in the wicket, but again Mushy is different. He is short. For him, bounce was never a big weapon. He bowls well on pitches with little bounce, bowling straight, bowling lots of overs and showing a great deal of patience.

'That is enough to get him a lot of wickets in county cricket. In the last season or two I think batsmen have tried to attack him more, with some success. But that just means that instead of getting five for 30 or 40 he's getting five for 80 or 90. But, crucially, he is still bowling people out.'

This is not a criticism of Warne, who has been wholehearted in his efforts for Hampshire and an inspirational captain to boot. But the fact that he has given his all for the cause and still been outperformed by Mushtaq is just one of the many aspects of this remarkable story.

One of the outstanding features of Mushtaq's career at Sussex has been his fitness. He is not one of the game's natural athletes (his liking for late-night curries does not help much) and he has been moving into portly middle-age for some years now. But he did not miss a match in his first three seasons at Hove, and missed only one game in each of the following two summers. Then there is his batting, which is not only hugely entertaining but also good enough to win a Test match – shown when he added 57 for the last wicket with Inzamam-ul-Haq to defeat Australia in Karachi in 1994–95.

Udal's assessment is generally echoed by Chris Adams, the Sussex captain, who was given the responsibility of getting the most out his match-winning new bowler, a bowler capable of running through sides on flat pitches.

Adams said: 'Mushy is not what I would call an explosive bowler, like Muttiah Muralitharan, who might take five for seven in five overs, although he can knock over the tail pretty quickly.

'He is not an extravagant turner of the ball. He doesn't give it a real rip, like Shane Warne. The majority of his wickets are lbw or bowled. That would suggest that he is not one of the biggest turners because if he was he would find it difficult to hit the stumps.

'But he's a master at bowling at the right pace, varying his flight and putting the ball in the difficult areas. His control is superb. His game is not so much about bowling magic balls, as tying batsmen down until they make errors.

'When he returned to Test cricket with Pakistan in the winter after his first summer with Sussex, he found it difficult to take wickets. But in that environment you have to take a wicket in six or seven overs or you're whipped off. I learned early on that I had to get him to bowl and bowl for him to get his returns.'

Mushtaq's success with Sussex has been observed with mixed feelings by Somerset's director of cricket, Brian Rose, a Taunton teammate of Mushtaq's in the 1990s. Mushtaq was a fine player for Somerset, but not as good as he has been over the past five years.

'What he has done for Sussex has been remarkable,' Rose said. 'At Somerset he was young and single and there were other things going on in his life. He's grown up.

'Technically, he's not much different. He's got great flight, great loop, getting the ball above the batsman's eye-level, which makes life difficult. He spins it less than some, but he's very accurate.

'I think the break from county and Test cricket did him good. He joined a county on the up, and he's been the number-one reason for their success. To win the Championship you need one bowler capable of taking 80-plus wickets in a season, and that's what he's done every year since joining Sussex.'

Mushtaq himself concedes that he is not a big spinner of the ball, but he said: 'I do turn it enough to worry batsmen and try to make it so they don't know which way I'm turning it. Lots of variation is my big thing, both with the pace of the ball and with my different actions. I bowl a leg-break with a googly action, for example. And I like a lot of overs to get into a rhythm.'

One of the players who first appreciated him at Hove was wicketkeeper Matt Prior, who said: 'It's his variation that is the key. He will float one up for the drive then bowl a quicker one that skids on. The googly is often aimed a little wider of the off-stump, to come in, while the leg-break drifts in towards the stumps through the air.

'Then he bowls the top-spinner and the flipper, changing his pace and his line. And then he will bowl them all again with different actions. For the batsman, it's a case of either hitting out and getting out, or going into a shell, surrounded by close catchers. There is a huge amount of pressure, and a lot of blokes end up being caught at bat-pad.'

He is, then, the captain's perfect bowler – one who will bowl long spells, giving control by keeping the runs down, while at the same time taking wickets on a remarkably consistent basis. The batsman often gets himself out. As the run-rate is squeezed and there seems no relief from the bowler, who whirrs in to deliver over after over, he will attempt to play a different stroke, to be more aggressive than he really wants to be.

It was not the first time that Sussex had looked to Asia for inspiration. Some of the county's most exotic cricketers, Ranjitsinhji, Duleepsinhji, Imran Khan, Javed Miandad and the Nawab of Pataudi, as dazzling as silk saris, have all performed at Hove. But none of them experienced the winning of the Championship. There was an important difference with Mushtaq. Here was a world-class spinner, and spin-bowling, historically, had been the county's weakness. Sussex have produced more than their fair share of dashing batsmen. Fast and fast-medium bowlers have been in plentiful supply, too, and there was no need to whistle down a mineshaft to find one, which was just as well. But spinners…

When, eventually, Sussex decided to go for a slow bowler, they identified the wrong men. Their first targets were the Australian leg-spinner Stuart MacGill and India's off-spinner Harbhajan Singh. It was only after Harbhajan had made it clear that he wanted to play for Lancashire, and MacGill had priced himself out of the market by reportedly asking for £100,000, that Sussex turned to Mushtaq. Sussex, as we have seen, have enjoyed the services of some of the game's most colourful cricketers. But when we look at their success in the overseas market, it is easy to overlook some of their clangers. In 1969 or 1970 Tony Greig had recommended a young batsman named Ken McEwan, who was living in Hove. No, said Sussex, we are signing an Indian off-spinner, Uday Joshi. McEwan became one of the finest of all overseas players, as Essex members would cheerfully confirm. When Imran Khan left Hove, he advised the county to have a look at an up-and-coming fast bowler called Waqar Younis. No, said Sussex, we are going to sign Tony Dodemaide. And they did.

Enthusiasm for Mushtaq, it must be said, was limited. He was 33 (at least!), he was not in the Pakistan side, and his career at Somerset had come to a less than glorious end some years before. He had even drifted out of the first-class game and had been playing League cricket in Staffordshire. But he did express enthusiasm and he felt he had something to prove. He had also proved his fitness by playing a couple of matches for Surrey in 2002, standing in for their regular overseas player Saqlain Mushtaq, who had gone to Morocco with the Pakistan team. Mushtaq, at a low point in his career, had spent the summer of 2002 living in Stoke-on-Trent and playing for League club Little Stoke, who paid him £12,500 for his services. He was short of money and had sold his car back in Pakistan.

The first of those games for Surrey was against Sussex at Hove. He failed to take a wicket in either innings, but generally bowled well. 'I bowled brilliantly,' said this normally modest man. 'But I did not get a wicket, and we lost the game.'

In the second match, he played at Leicester, in front of John Major, and had figures of 5–71 and 3–115 as Surrey won by seven wickets. Leicestershire contacted him and said that they wanted to sign him as their overseas player for 2003, but that their first priority was to sign a good seamer, and they would get back to him after that. Sussex acted more quickly. They consulted Keith Medlycott, then the Surrey coach, who said he had been impressed by the player in his brief stint at the club. The Sussex management convinced themselves that this was their man. He had, after all, performed successfully at the highest level (183 wickets in 50 Tests at that time). He had, on his day, earned the right to stand alongside Warne and Anil Kumble as one of the three foremost wrist-spinners in the world game. Mark Taylor, the former Australian captain, had described Mushtaq as the greatest leg-spinner he had ever seen.

Sussex signed him – and for about half the money that MacGill's representatives had been asking for. They thought he would be good. They did not know how good.

Mushtaq said: 'Peter [the Sussex coach, Peter Moores] made a big gamble by offering me a job, and I felt determined to repay him. And I always wanted to get 100 wickets in a season. It was something very special for me. I had gone close before, at Somerset, but with 95 wickets and one match to go I got a fever and missed the game.'

How Leicestershire must regret their dilatoriness in 2002. Mushtaq returned to Grace Road in July 2003 to taunt them with figures of 5–93 and 5–96. Then, at the end of the season, Leicestershire were the opponents as Sussex won the Championship. Leicestershire finished bottom of the table, were relegated and have failed to return to the top level of the four-day game. But things did not start well for Mushtaq in 2003. Sussex were beaten by Middlesex at Lord's in their opening game (Mushtaq 3–16 and 1–97). Adams, however, was far from discouraged.

'After Lord's we knew we had what we'd been looking for for so long – the X-factor. We knew that in Mushy we had someone to work around. He had been suffering with a septic nail in the second innings, and it was amazing he could even hold the ball, let alone bowl it.'

Mushtaq made his home debut for Sussex at Hove at the end of April. Kent, an ancient enemy, were the opposition, and they were beaten by 133 runs. James Kirtley was the Sussex star, with figures of 6–26 in Kent's second innings. Mushtaq's contribution had been steady, with three wickets in each innings and a useful knock of 37, without being the stuff of headlines.

In the next match, against Warwickshire at Edgbaston, Mushtaq took six wickets in the first innings, but they cost 157 runs, and Sussex went on to lose the match. It was their second defeat in three matches and Peter Moores was very critical of his players. Mushtaq played a critical role off the field at Edgbaston. He spoke to the players, telling them not to talk about 'him' or 'I' anymore but to use 'we' when winning or losing. His English was not the best, but he came across to the other players as a dedicated team man.

It was in the next Championship game at home, against Nottinghamshire at Horsham, that Sussex discovered that they really did have a bowler capable of propelling them to their first title. This was the match in which Kevin Innes made history as the first 12th man in first-class cricket to score a century. Under new regulations, James Kirtley, who had been released from the England squad, could replace a nominated player in the Sussex side. But before he did so, that player, Innes, had been required to bat, and he responded with his maiden century in a Sussex score of 619–7 declared.

Mushtaq took some punishment from the young Kevin Pietersen, who reached his century from only 75 balls. But he still took six wickets to make Notts follow-on. And when they did so, he took six wickets in the second innings too, this time for 81, to give him a match analysis of 12–244, the best by a Sussex spinner since Eddie Hemmings, at the age of 44, took 12–58, also at Horsham. When, at the end of June, Mushtaq took 11 wickets against Warwickshire to banish memories of their embarrassing surrender in Birmingham, he already had 52 in only seven Championship matches, and there was growing speculation that he would become the first bowler to take 100 wickets in an English season since Andy Caddick and Courtney Walsh both managed the feat in 1998.

Talk of winning the Championship had been banned in the Sussex dressing room, but the players were thinking about it all the same, and even more so after they beat Essex at Arundel and then Leicestershire at Grace Road to trim Surrey's lead to just five points. They could have gone top of the table with their fifth consecutive win in the next match at Trent Bridge, but it was a damp draw and Mushtaq took only two wickets.

The next match, against Surrey at Hove, brought in record gate receipts of over £20,000. The match between the top two was a crucial fixture. But it was a draw, and Chris Adams was attacked for delaying his declaration, setting Surrey a notional target of 377 in 34 overs; Mushtaq took four wickets in the first innings.

In the next game, an equally important fixture at home to Lancashire, Mushtaq was back to his best with match figures of 11–173 as Sussex won by 252 runs with just 12 minutes to spare. Again, Adams appeared guilty of conservatism, delaying his declaration until 12.35 on the last day. He was almost inch-perfect. Mushtaq was the key player in the final session, taking 5–23 in 17.2 overs with seven fielders round the bat. Peter Moores and the rest of the coaching staff placed themselves round the boundary to 'field' the boundaries and ensure the swift return of the ball.

Sussex moved to the top of the table for the first time when, in their next match, they beat Essex at Colchester by an innings and 120 runs, and Mushtaq, with four wickets in the first innings and three in the second, was once again a pivotal figure. With three matches to go Sussex were now the leaders and favourites to win the title. And if there was one match that defined their summer – and their character – it was their next home game against Middlesex, when Mushtaq played a key role with the bat. Sussex were 107 for six in reply to Middlesex's 392 (Mushtaq 6–145) and looked certain to follow-on. But, in the most important partnership of the season, Matt Prior (148) and Mark Davis (168) put on 195 for the seventh wicket. When Prior was out, Mushtaq clumped a merry 57 as he put on 97 with Davis to nudge Sussex past the Middlesex total.

Mushtaq went to Old Trafford for the penultimate match of the season needing just one wicket for his 100. And for the first time in the season he failed to take one. Sussex could have won the title there but paid for their safety-first approach and lost by an innings and 19 runs. Mushtaq made another fifty, but Sussex missed his wickets.

And so, on to Hove and history. Sussex needed six points from their last game against Leicestershire to put themselves beyond Lancashire's desperate grasp. They took 22, winning by an innings and 55 runs to take the title with some style, equalling Surrey's First Division record of 10 victories. Mushtaq was so nervous that he arrived for the match on Wednesday morning without his whites, which he had left in his kitchen. A driver who did not care about speed limits was sent to get them. Mushtaq took his 100th of the season with the first of his four wickets in the first innings. It came with the last delivery before lunch on the opening day, when he bowled Brad Hodge with a leg-break. He was injured and unable to bowl in Leicestershire's second innings, which is probably why the ultimate victory was delayed on the Friday. This was, and always will be, the highlight of Mushtaq's career in county cricket.

Mushtaq Ahmed removes Brad Hodge of Leicestershire to take his 100th first-class wicket in 2003.

Mushtaq Ahmed celebrates his 100th wicket of the 2003 season.

The season of 2004 was a disappointment, and for a while it seemed that Sussex might get relegated. At the halfway point of the season they had won only one first-class match. Mushtaq's form mirrored that of the side. Halfway through the season he had taken a modest 30 wickets. But he then took 23 in consecutive victories over Middlesex and Worcestershire and, from nowhere, Sussex suddenly had an outside chance of retaining their title. Against Worcestershire, his figures were 6–67 and 7–73 to give him an overall return of 13–140, his best match analysis in England. His total of 84 wickets was well down on the previous year, but he was the country's leading wicket-taker for the second consecutive year, repeating the feat of Derek Underwood in 1979.

Tim Ambrose stumps Leicestershire's John Sadler to give Mushtaq Ahmed another wicket in the title-clincher in September 2003. Tony Cottey admires his handiwork from slip.

All lit up. Mushtaq Ahmed puffs away at the celebration to mark Sussex's first Championship success.

In 2005, the year which brought the curtain down on Peter Moores's time at Hove, Sussex went close to winning the title again; they finished third behind Nottinghamshire and Hampshire. With better luck with the weather and a bit more of Rana Naved, who took 54 wickets in only nine Championship matches, the title would surely have been theirs. Mushtaq took 80 wickets, to take his total to 267 in three astonishing seasons. At the end of the season he was offered a

As well as his bowling, Mushtaq Ahmed is no mug with the bat, as he shows against Kent at Hove in September 2005.

That's got to be out? Mushtaq Ahmed appeals against Middlesex at Lord's.

Mushtaq Ahmed in action against Hampshire.

fresh two-year contract. In 2006, when Sussex were again champions, Mushtaq was their key player once more. He took 102 wickets, one fewer than in 2003, but he missed a match and bowled 213 fewer overs. He saved his best until last, returning a career-best 9–48 against Nottinghamshire at Trent Bridge in September to give himself match figures of 13 for 108.

There were 90 more wickets in 2007, as Sussex retained the title after shaky performances against Warwickshire and

Kent at the start of the season. By now, batsmen around the county circuit were attempting to hit Mushtaq out of his match-winning rhythm, but they rarely profited from their more aggressive methods. He has always been an attacking bowler. In his foreword to Mushtaq's autobiography, *Twenty20 Vision,* his former Pakistan captain Imran Khan says: 'Mushtaq's own natural, attacking instincts were what really made him stand out and what compelled me as captain to stick by him in the face of opposition from selectors and even teammates.

'The fact that he was an adventurous player made me insist on his selection for the World Cup of 1992. Mushtaq is a cricketer who is never afraid to lose, and as such he has the potential to win games for you from apparently hopeless positions.

'Midway through the 1992 World Cup we were 50–1 outsiders. Our Final victory was an incredible comeback, and I used Mushtaq, as well as Wasim and Aaqib Javed, to attack, and I let them know I did not care how many runs they conceded.

'Mushtaq's googly to dismiss Graeme Hick in the Final is one of the great moments in Pakistan cricket.'

There is a suspicion that most Pakistan cricketers are a little older than Methuselah. Certainly, a birth certificate has often represented a basis for negotiation to establish a player's age, rather than a document of unshakeable truth. Parents of aspiring cricketers have often pretended that their sons are younger than they really are in order to improve their chances of adolescent progress. But if we are to believe Mushtaq's certificate, he was born in Sahiwal, a city in the south-east of the Punjab province and a two-hour drive from Lahore, on 28 June 1970. He was one of 10 children, five boys and five girls, though he lost a brother and a sister when he was young. His father, Shamsudin, was a cotton worker who earned a pound a day, starting at five in the morning and getting home at midnight. All the money he earned was spent on food and clothes. He died in 2004, the year after his son joined Sussex.

Shamsudin discouraged his son's passion for cricket, emphasising the importance of education, but it was a hopeless battle. Mushtaq was so potty about the game that he would sometimes practise through the night. When he slept, he did so with a cricket ball beside him. When he played, he pretended he was Abdul Qadir when he bowled leg-spin and Imran Khan when he bowled medium-pace. He taught himself accuracy by bowling to a tree – when he missed his target he had to run after the ball to retrieve it.

Truancy was a problem. 'I missed a lot of schooling to play cricket,' he wrote in *Twenty20 Vision.* 'The teacher eventually called my father to ask where I had been.

'It must have been very embarrassing for him because he believed I had been attending classes, and he was shocked to find out I had not been there for such a long time.

'My father took me aside and asked me, "How is your education going?" I said, "Fine, absolutely brilliant. I'm doing a great job at school." So he said, "Well, as you're doing such a good job, why not have an extra tuition after school so you can really succeed?"

'I said, "No, I really don't need it." I was feeling really guilty, and I knew I was in big trouble when he took me on his bike to see the teacher. They both beat me until one of the sticks actually broke on me.'

On another occasion he skipped school to watch the touring West Indies play the Rest of Punjab in Sahiwal, even running under a moving train to get to the ground to glimpse Viv Richards, Gordon Greenidge, Malcolm Marshall and Sylvester Clarke. He was a good hockey player, quick and with dribbling skills, and his brother, Ishfaq, who was vice-captain, put him in the team for one match when they were short of players.

One of his teachers was impressed with his performance and suggested that he could also help out the cricket team when they were a player short.

'He asked me if I would be 12th man, and I agreed very happily. At the nets before the match they asked me to bowl at the batsmen, and I bowled leg-breaks. I was spinning the ball big time and getting wickets. So the teachers picked me to play, and I used to pick up three or four wickets every game.'

The story of how his father was finally won over is quite moving. In *Twenty20 Vision* Mushtaq says: 'My father eventually relented after I had been playing for a couple of years, and he offered me his unconditional support.

'It was a wonderful moment for me when he took me on his bicycle to the nearest shop selling cricket gear. I was about 13 years old, and he bought me a cricket bat for 300 rupees, which was about £3 at the time.

'This was a lot of money for him, and it meant everything to me. I showed it to everyone for days and went on to use the bat for the next couple of years. My father then started to watch me play and enjoyed the games, but I felt immense pressure when he was there, and I struggled to get the same satisfaction as before.

'I would be very scared, and it affected me so much that I asked him to stop coming to watch me. I felt that if I failed I was letting him down, and it would be a disappointment to him. He agreed to stop watching me but, little did I know, he was actually turning up and viewing games from a distance or even from behind a tree.'

His big break came, he says, when he was picked to play against the bigger, better-equipped Comprehensive High School, the main local rivals, in the district Final. He took 4–80 in 25 overs and the opposition invited him to play for them. When the High School offered to buy him a bicycle, as they were four miles away, he decided to make the move.

There were problems at the new school. The young Mushtaq spoke Punjabi, and the 'more refined' Urdu was the official language of the school. He felt that he did not fit in, while his old friends teased him with such jibes as 'Mushy is easy to buy.' But he won over his new schoolmates with his talent in cricket, with both bat and ball. He was made captain of the Comprehensive High School and then invited to play for Montgomery Cricket Club, owned by Bisharat Shafi, who was also president of the Multan Cricket Division.

He was only 15 when he first played for the Multan Under-19 side and, still unable to bowl the googly or the flipper, was regarded as much for his batting as his bowling. He made 75 on his debut. Beside him, Inzamam-ul-Haq scored a century.

By the time he was 16, Mushtaq was captain of the side, which included not only Inzy but a fast bowler called Waqar Younis. He was now playing first-class cricket, and he became a precocious star at 17 when he played against Mike Gatting's touring side.

This was the tour made infamous by its appalling umpiring. Mushtaq had been named as the 14th man in the squad for the match between England and a Punjab Chief Minister's XI in his home town of Sahiwal. He was told he would be the water boy for the team and that his duties would be to look after the team and carry the kit.

'Then Salim Malik came over to me and said, "Mushtaq, young fellow, you are playing today." I was speechless. I was truly amazed. I marvelled that I was going to be playing against John Emburey, Derek Randall and David Capel. I kept telling myself I was going to play in a match with Tim Robinson! I was not nervous – I was flying. I did not even have my kit with me, and I had not brought any spikes.

'It was only my second or third first-class match, and I never found out why I was picked. It was an incredible game. I bowled 36 overs and took 6–85 in the first innings, and I remember dismissing Robinson, Bill Athey, Capel and Phil Defreitas.

'When I came off the pitch there were cameras flashing everywhere, and the English media were asking me to stand to one side and have my photo taken. I was overwhelmed. It was an experience I will never forget, especially as I had turned up really only to hold the drinks.'

It got better. When his hero, Abdul Qadir, fell out with the Pakistan Cricket Board, he was called up to play in the third Test against England in Karachi, though before he had the chance to play Qadir had resolved his differences with the board and had rejoined the team. But Mushtaq was immediately offered a full-time contract with United Bank. He was on his way as a full-time first-class cricketer. He hit the headlines again in 1988 when he took 19 wickets in the 1988 Youth World Cup in Australia. In the domestic season of 1988–89 he took 52 wickets, and he took 26 wickets at 19.76 in an Under-19 series against India. He first played for Pakistan in a one-day match in Sharjah in March 1989, and in 1990 he made his Test debut in Adelaide after being flown out to replace Qadir. Mushtaq finished with figures of 1–141 from 48 overs and muffed a return catch offered by Dean Jones, who scored a century in each innings and used his feet cleverly to counter the leg-spinner.

It did not get any better. In the next match, against Victoria in Melbourne, he was twice warned by umpire Robin Bailhache for following through down the pitch. When he continued to do so, he was withdrawn from the attack by the umpires, and the Pakistan players refused to accept the decision and walked off the pitch, though they eventually returned. Mushtaq took just five wickets in the series and they came in at 42.40 each. But better times were not far away. By the time of the 1992 World Cup he had become a key figure in captain Imran's one-day plans, and in the tournament he took 16 wickets. His figures in the Final, when Pakistan beat England by 22 runs, were 3–41.

'I was so happy to win the World Cup with Imran Khan as captain because he was the man who changed my career. I remember being expensive and not taking the wickets and Imran came over to me, put his arm round my shoulders and told me to always be brave.

'He told me that I could always win matches, but that I should not be afraid if people hit me. It was a big boost. That was when I decided to go for it whenever I bowled and not to be afraid to buy wickets.'

When Mushtaq came to England in 1992, Imran had gone. But he still formed, with Wasim Akram and Waqar Younis, one of the Pakistan's finest attacks. He took 15 wickets at 31.66, and down in Somerset important people began to take note.

'The whole process of signing him took about five minutes,' recalled Rose. 'Mushy was so keen to come, and he was the model overseas player. He won matches for the club and brought in the members.

He was Somerset's Player of the Year in his first season with the club, 1993. He took 85 first-class wickets at 20.85 and scored almost 500 runs. Somerset, like Sussex eight years later, started thinking about winning their first Championship. From 1985–92 they had finished 17th, 16th, 11th, 11th, 14th, 15th, 17th and 9th. In 1993 they were fifth.

Peter Anderson, the county's chief executive at the time, said: 'Mushy was a pure joy. He was a bubbly, extrovert character at the County Ground, who was as popular off the field as he was on it. He loved talking cricket and often held court after matches.

'The younger players lapped it up because he was a Test star. At Taunton the wickets were designed to suit Andy Caddick in those days, but it didn't matter to Mush. He could bowl on any wicket. There was some bounce for him here, though, and he made the most of that.'

But 1993 also marked a low point in his life. During Pakistan's tour of the West Indies he showed he was in prime form with the ball, taking 5–86 and 3–43 in the 114-run win over Jamaica and 6–43 against the Under-23 side in Grenada. But it was in the course of this match that he was arrested, along with Wasim, Waqar and Aaqib Javed, on charges of 'constructive possession of a banned drug.' He was released when the charge was dropped but missed the first Test because of a back injury.

Mushtaq may appear to be one of the most exuberant of cricketers, but he has experienced enough set-backs over the years to wipe the smile from his face. There were those drug allegations in 1993, and he also played for Pakistan at the time of the match-fixing charges in the 1990s. He was fined £3,000, and it was recommended that he should never be made captain of his country, or even a selector. He protested his innocence, as he does to this day. He was also with the Pakistan team in Jamaica during the 2007 World Cup when the team coach, Bob Woolmer, was found dead – thought murdered – in his hotel room.

All that was a long way away as he prepared for the 1994 season in England. Hopes were high at Taunton in 1994 after the previous summer, but the club lost their first eight competitive matches. Andy Caddick and Neil Mallender were injured. Mushtaq did well enough, taking 40 wickets in only eight matches, but Pakistan demanded his return earlier than expected for the tour of Sri Lanka.

Me again. Mushtaq Ahmed celebrates another wicket and an unusual trophy of his latest victim.

He made up for that disappointment in 1995. He took 95 first-class wickets, his best return until the heady summer of 2003, and he took five or more wickets in an innings on seven occasions. He bowled so many googlies that Martin Crowe suggested that batsmen should play him as an off-spinner and some county players even nicknamed him 'Tauseef' after the Pakistan off-spinner. But he kept taking wickets. He took 58 wickets in the seven matches Somerset won and bowled more overs, 952, than anyone else in the country. But for an injury to Caddick, who played just six Championship games, and a collapse in form of the two opening batsmen, Marcus Trescothick and Mark Lathwell, a title challenge would have been sustained. He did not play for Pakistan in 1996, when he toured England with the Pakistan team and finished above Wasim and Waqar in the bowling averages, taking 17 wickets in the three Tests at 26.29.

In the first Test at Lord's, where Michael Atherton and Alec Stewart threatened to save the match for England, Mushtaq was responsible for their collapse from 168–1 to 243 all out. He finished with figures of 5–57. On the last day of The Oval Test he bowled 30 overs unchanged from the Vauxhall End and took 6–67. His captain, Wasim Akram, declared that he was a better bowler than Warne.

He was one of Wisden's Five Cricketers of the Year in the 1997 almanack, and Vic Marks, a Somerset spinner of another generation, was fulsome in his praise.

'By taking 45 wickets in six Tests for Pakistan between November 1995 and August 1996 Mushtaq Ahmed confirmed his status as the final member – alongside Shane Warne and Anil Kumble – of a glittering triumvirate of wrist-spinners who adorn the modern game,' he said. 'Mushtaq is the most enchanting of the lot. He is the arch-deceiver, possessing every nefarious variation in the wrist-spinner's armoury. Unlike the others he has a googly which is indecipherable to most international batsmen.'

After 1996, though, there was a decline. And it had a rather sombre, terminal whiff about it. He returned to Taunton in 1997 but looked jaded after another busy international winter. He could hardly be judged a failure, for he took 50 wickets in 14 Championship matches at 28 runs apiece. But he was not the match-winner of two summers before and was troubled by a knee injury. If 1997 was a little disappointing, 1998 was a total let-down. He played in only six Championship matches and took 14 wickets with a best return of 3–26. He was worried about his wife's confinement, and that knee injury was still a problem. He had lost his place in the Pakistan side and, significantly, his good humour had deserted him.

He remembered: 'I had played for Somerset for four years and they were good ones. But what happened in 1998 was my fault, and I regret it very much. There was a change of coach, which did not help. But I must take the blame.

'I didn't have a good time. Mentally, I was just not there. But I was very upset to be away from my family at a difficult time. I would say that my last season with Somerset was the first time in my career that I wasn't really enjoying my cricket, and enjoying it is very important to me. Because I am a professional, I have to consider the money. But I really love playing the game.

'When there is rain I hate it. Some cricketers like having a rest in the dressing room, but I do not because it destroys my opportunity to play cricket. How can you say that you are the best spinner in the world when you are sitting in the dressing room? But that last year at Somerset was the only time I didn't have my usual feeling about the game.'

In his book, *Twenty20 Vision*, he goes into more detail and reveals that his career was not helped by the arrival of Dermot Reeve.

'Dermot took over as coach in 1997 and brought some new ideas about the way we should eat, train and play cricket. I did not accept his ideas.

'It may be that I was not ready for the changes, or perhaps that I did not appreciate the way that he introduced them, but I was not right in myself, and it was easy to make excuses for my performances by blaming the coach.

'I can see that I was not always interpreting Dermot's behaviour correctly. He always tried to keep the atmosphere light and make jokes, and sometimes he would appear to put me down in team meetings. When I stood up to make a point he would say something like "Can you understand his English?" to my teammates. At the time I saw it as an insult.'

Mushtaq was an unhappy man on and off the field. 'After matches in Taunton I would go home for a meal and then go out again. I would insist that I needed to socialise to help team spirit. That was just an excuse that I made up to justify living a selfish life. My life had no meaning at this time.

'The 1998 season began in exactly the same way. I was desperately unhappy, although I could not tell anybody. I even tried throwing the ball up in the air a few time to let it drop on to my spinning finger so I could get an injury. I was living a bad life and making myself unhappy.'

He had a number of meetings with the chief executive during this time. 'I told Peter Anderson that I wanted to go home. I asked him to forgive me and explained that I did not want any money. I said that I had tried my level best to stay as long as I could. I described myself as an empty man and told him that could not help myself or Somerset and I had to leave. He agreed, and I returned to Pakistan as soon as possible.

'I cannot think of a worse way to leave Taunton. The county has a long history and many great players have represented Somerset over the years. Men such as Viv Richards, Sunil Gavaskar, Joel Garner and Ian Botham were highly respected, and I believe that I received similar respect when I was there. Playing county cricket had helped me to move from thinking that I was a back-up bowler to Wasim and Waqar to believing that I was a match-winner. For this I will always be grateful.'

Luckily, Somerset members did not hold a grudge against Mushtaq. Perhaps it was because there had been a suitable gap between his two county careers, but when he returned to Taunton at the end of the 2003, he was welcomed like a prodigal son.

Anderson said: 'When he came down with Sussex he received a wonderful welcome from everyone. Because of what he had achieved and because everyone loved him. And if he apologised to me once, he apologised a hundred times for the way his career tailed off.

Sussex followers spell out their support for the brilliant Mushtaq Ahmed.

'I think he got distracted with a few things that were happening off the field with Pakistan cricket. There were accusations of gambling with some players. It was difficult for him. And he enjoyed a drink or two at the time.

'But, overall, we remember him most fondly for making such a big impact in his few years at Taunton. And even more than his marvellous leg-breaks I remember his enthusiasm, the fact that he really wanted to play. That's something you can't say about all county cricketers.

'He has settled down as a mature family man, and he seems to be taking his religion even more seriously these days. It's all helping his cricket.'

When Mushtaq returned to Pakistan in 1998, his religion became more important to him. 'Between 1998 and 2000, Inzamam, Shahid Afridi and many other cricketers changed their lives too. When we toured England in 2001 the whole team would spend time visiting mosques, praying together, listening to scholars describing the life of the Prophet Muhammad and giving to charity.'

There were beards everywhere. But praying did not help Mushtaq get back into the Pakistan team. He topped the tour bowling averages in 2001 with 14 wickets at 12 each, but he did not get into the Test side. When he was dropped from the one-day side, he even went to Manchester looking to play in League cricket to help pay for his wife and family, who were with him. For a little over a month he played for Northop Hall in Chester.

When he returned to Pakistan that winter he became captain of National Bank, and they won the

PCB Patron's Trophy that season. But as the English season approached, and his wife, Uzma, gave birth to their third child, Habiba, he was full of fresh worries.

'In 2002 I could not get a contract in England. My time at Somerset had ended badly and no first-class teams wanted me. Even Premier League cricket was out of the question because the clubs could not afford me.'

It was then that his agent, Gary Mellor, arranged for him to receive £12,500 to play for Little Stoke. Then Surrey, then Sussex, then immortality. The Sussex success story in recent summers is about many things. It is about an inspiring coach and a driving captain. It is about the batting of Murray Goodwin and the team spirit that comes from a small, close-knit and fiercely focused squad. But, more than anything else, it has been about the little man with the black beard prancing in to bowl yet another delivery which, invariably, will be followed by a bellowed appeal. Umpires do not like it when Mushy is bowling because he works them harder than any other bowler in the world game.

Mushtaq Ahmed is presented with the ball with which he completed his 100th five-wicket haul in first-class cricket in August 2007.

Chapter 4
It's All About the Players

IF SUSSEX'S astonishing success over the last six seasons has proved one thing, it is that less is most definitely more. Over the three Championships and various one-day successes during that time the county have used a modest 29 players. When their first Championship was secured in 2003, some counties were still operating with bloated playing staffs close to that number in a season.

Not Sussex. In 2003, his fifth season as coach, Peter Moores made a conscious decision that quality rather than quantity was the way forward. He would operate with a squad of just 18 professionals – easily the smallest number among the 18 first-class counties. In his first year as coach the number had been 24, although that was still small compared with many of Sussex's rivals. They would all be regarded as potential first-team players, salaries would be competitive (although do not get the impression that a first-year pro was earning much more than the minimum wage) and there were attractive bonuses for any success achieved – as Sussex's insurers were to discover.

'We believed in rewarding the players well,' said Moores. 'But as well as having talent – which every professional cricketer has – they had to buy in to what we were trying to achieve in every aspect of the game.'

So did the backroom staff. Of course the days when counties operated with a single behind-the-scenes dogsbody, whose duties would include everything from massage to sweeping out the dressing rooms and running errands to the bookies, disappeared with the era of Denis Compton and Fred Trueman. Moores knew that if he was to keep his best 11 players on the pitch throughout the gruelling slog that the county season has become, he needed the best backroom team he could get.

'That was as important as the playing side, and fortunately the guys behind the scenes – physios Stuart Osborne and James Carmichael and physiologist Ben Haining – bought in to what we were trying to achieve.'

Of the 15 players who helped secure Sussex's first Championship, six played in all 16 matches: skipper Chris Adams, Mushtaq Ahmed, Richard Montgomerie, Murray Goodwin, Robin Martin-Jenkins and Matt Prior. Tim Ambrose and Tony Cottey missed just one match each. There was little change three years later, when 17 players were used. One, Duncan Spencer, played in the opening game before quietly disappearing, while Andrew Hodd appeared twice. There were five ever-presents: Adams, Goodwin, Montgomerie, Carl Hopkinson and Jason Lewry, while Mushtaq Ahmed missed just one game – the only Championship fixture he has not played in during his time at Hove – and Martin-Jenkins and Prior were both absent for two matches.

In 2007 Sussex secured back-to-back titles with 18 players out of a slightly larger playing staff of 19 professionals. But five of those played in four games or fewer, while Adams, Mushtaq and Chris Nash played in every match. Goodwin missed the title clincher against Worcestershire because of a family bereavement, while the horrific shoulder injury he suffered in the penultimate match at Durham robbed Rana Naved-ul-Hasan of his ever-present record.

Eight players have been generic to all three titles – Adams, Mushtaq, Goodwin, James Kirtley, Lewry, Martin-Jenkins, Montgomerie and Mike Yardy. The remarkable Adams has played in each of Sussex's 79 Championship matches since the start of 2003 – proof, if any were needed, of his remarkable fitness and mental strength. Mind you, he did get one match off – the game against Surrey at The Oval in August 2007 was abandoned without a ball being bowled.

Of course, not all the players who have been at Sussex since their first title have enjoyed Championship glory. Opening batsman Ian Ward was recruited in 2004 in the hope that his experience and proven record would help Sussex retain their title. For his part, the likeable Ward felt a move to the South Coast might revive his chances of an England recall – he had won the last of his five Test caps in 2001. But the left-hander fulfilled just two seasons of his three-year contract before accepting a lucrative offer to become a full-time cricket presenter on Sky Sports.

Ward finished his Sussex career with a respectable average nudging 40, but even he admitted when it was all over that the county did not get the best out of him. At Hove, where the slow pitches were totally alien to a player who gilded his reputation on the quicker, bouncier Oval wickets, it was a real struggle. Ward made five hundreds with a top score of 160, but confessed that he might not have joined Sussex had he known how much of a struggle playing at headquarters would become. He missed nearly half of his second season through a combination of neck and groin injuries, to add to the sense that he had failed to do himself justice. 'When the TV offer came along I knew it was going to be a really hard decision to make because I was still contracted to Sussex,' he said.

'The club were fantastic about everything, and Mark Robinson was especially supportive. I really enjoyed my time at Sussex and I'm disappointed I wasn't able to make more of a contribution in

Ian Ward had two seasons with Sussex before retiring to take up a career as a presenter with Sky Sports.

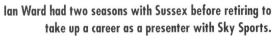

Mohammad Akram left after just one season with Sussex to join Surrey.

South African Johan van der Wath had a short stint as overseas player in 2005.

2005, especially as I had hardly ever missed a game up until then in my career.

'That was very frustrating, but in my two years I got a glimpse of what makes the county so special. They are a great county, and the camaraderie in the dressing room is what defines Sussex.'

Ward is in a very small group of just three players who have not had a role, however peripheral, in what Sussex have achieved in their golden age. The others are Mohammad Akram, who joined Surrey after just one fairly average season at Hove in 2005, and Johan van der Wath.

Akram arrived in 2004 with a reputation for being something of an unfulfilled talent. Sussex had been impressed with him the previous year when he played a few games for Essex as he tried to secure English qualification and took five wickets – including Adams for a duck – in a losing cause as Sussex won by an innings at Colchester on their way to their first Championship. He was capable of bowling high-quality spells of fast bowling, but Sussex only glimpsed his mercurial talents on occasions. Indeed, he will be remembered more for having to vehemently protest his innocence after Sussex were caught up in a ball-tampering row against Warwickshire at Horsham in June 2005, when they were deducted five penalty runs by umpires Peter Willey and Barrie Leadbeater – the first instance in Sussex's history since the punishment was introduced.

A few weeks later, Akram had to be taken out of the attack for bowling a beamer in a match against Lancashire, ironically after a quality spell in the first innings had set up a rare Sussex win at Old Trafford. His desire to play for a county closer to his London home was fulfilled when Surrey came in for him at the end of the season, and he was released halfway through his two-year contract, but he remained an unfulfilled talent at The Oval and was released by Surrey at the end of the 2007 season.

Johan van der Wath was the swarthy South African whose second spell in English cricket with Northamptonshire has been more successful than the few weeks he spent at Hove in 2005. Signed as a short-term locum before Rana Naved joined the county, he played in four Championship games but only took four expensive wickets. Van der Wath's explosive talents were more suited to the one-day game, where he bowled with consistent hostility and could hit the ball a long way. One game in particular stood out when he smashed 73 off 43 balls against Somerset at Taunton as Sussex pulled off a remarkable triumph.

It was no surprise to Sussex watchers that he forged a successful one-day international career for his country, nor that his second spell in English cricket has been much more productive. In nine Championship games for Northamptonshire in 2007 he took 29 wickets at 27.06 – the best figures by any seamer at Wantage Road that season.

Some of the other 26 have moved on since helping Sussex to glory and, as we will discover, a few are no longer involved in the professional game at all.

Tim Ambrose (2001–05)

The irony was not lost on Sussex supporters when Tim Ambrose realised a long-held dream to play for England early in 2008. During his five seasons at Hove, Ambrose and Matt Prior were rivals for the wicketkeeper-batsman's role. Ambrose was first choice when Sussex won their first Championship in 2003,

but eventually Peter Moores opted for his rival and two years after leaving Sussex he picked Prior again when he selected his first squad as the new England coach. Prior played in 10 consecutive Test matches but lost his place at the start of 2008 – to Ambrose.

Sussex had struggled to find a wicketkeeper who could contribute consistent runs since Moores retired in 1998. Shaun Humphries and Nick Wilton were both excellent glove men, but neither made a first-class hundred. Prior arrived on the staff in 2001 through conventional routes – he had first worked with Moores as a 12-year-old when he joined Sussex's junior set-up – but the same could not be said of Ambrose. In fact, had it not been for the persistence of an aunt in Seaford, he might have been lost to Sussex, and English, cricket forever.

Tim Ambrose won a Championship-winners' medal in 2003 but left Sussex to join Warwickshire two years later.

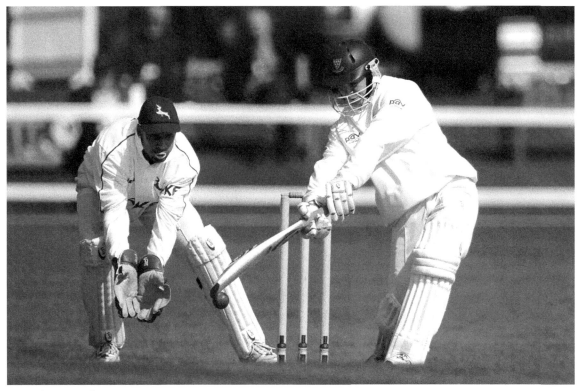

Tim Ambrose cuts loose.

Ambrose was building a reputation as one of the best young players in his native New South Wales and was keen to broaden his cricket horizons. His English mother, Sally, asked her sister on the Sussex coast if she could make some enquiries, and in the spring of 2000 a letter arrived at Eastbourne CC which was picked up by cricket manager Peter Bibby.

'We knew he was in the New South Wales development squad and was obviously a talented player, but I must admit that the thing which impressed us most was that he would not cost us anything,' recalled Bibby.

Ambrose made his debut on a chilly April Saturday at the Saffrons and scored 42 in a Sussex League match against East Grinstead. He finished the season as the club's leading scorer with more than 600 runs and it was not long before Eastbourne realised they had a talent on their hands, even though at that stage Ambrose played primarily as a specialist batsman and rarely pulled on the gauntlets. The jungle drums were soon beating and Moores was alerted. Within two months Ambrose was making his second-team debut for Sussex. He played in five games that season, but only kept in a couple of them. His teammates included Prior and Hugo Southwell, who these days is an integral part of the Scotland rugby side.

Ambrose did enough to convince Sussex that he was worth a contract and he joined the staff in 2001, but he never forgot his roots. Five years later he was still turning out for Eastbourne when he could and even scored a century on his last appearance for them, against Steyning.

'When he signed, Mooresy reckoned he was the best young player in England, which was some accolade,' said Bibby. 'He was a fantastic chap who would do anything for anyone.'

In their first season as rivals Prior had the edge and Ambrose waited until September before marking his Championship debut with a composed half-century against Warwickshire as Sussex got the draw that virtually secured promotion to Division One. Such was the rate of his development that by 2003 he was first-choice keeper and impressing everyone with his neat and tidy glove-work and crucial contributions at number five, not least the unbeaten 93 against Essex at Arundel which gave Sussex the belief that they could win the Championship. It was one of eight half-centuries that summer.

At 21 Ambrose had become a Championship-winner and, having declared his intention to play for England rather than Australia when he became qualified by residency in 2004, he looked to have a long and successful future at Hove. He started 2004 with a half-century against Surrey, but his form, as with so many of his teammates as Sussex made a stuttering title defence, deserted him. His next 10 Championship innings yielded just 92 runs, even though he swapped places with Prior in the batting order and dropped down to number six. After his third duck of the season, against Gloucestershire at Arundel in June, he lost his place and Prior took over the gloves.

Ambrose's frustrations intensified in 2005. He played in only five Championship games and kept wicket in just one of them when Prior was called into the England one-day squad. Sussex were desperate to hang on to him and offered him an improved two-year contract, but they were fighting a losing battle.

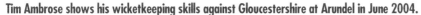

Tim Ambrose shows his wicketkeeping skills against Gloucestershire at Arundel in June 2004.

Ambrose knew that if he was to fulfil his ambition of keeping wicket for England he needed to be playing every week. Warwickshire made him a good offer and in October 2005 he joined the Bears, the county Ambrose had made both his second-team and first-class debuts against. At the end of 2007 he extended his contract at Edgbaston, and a few weeks later, after some impressive performances for the England Academy team in India, he had replaced his friendly rival Prior in the Test squad.

Self-effacing is not a characteristic generally associated with Australian sportsmen, but it was no surprise when he talked about his selection that Ambrose's thoughts soon turned to the man he had replaced. They were rivals at Hove but remained firm friends, and no one was more thrilled when Prior announced himself on the Test scene with such style in 2007. It might have helped both players improve had they been rivals again in New Zealand.

Ambrose has never forgotten his roots, either. He still regards the people he met when he arrived in Eastbourne as a wet-behind-the-ears 17-year-old as friends.

'Leaving Sussex was probably the hardest decision I will ever have to make in my career,' he said. 'It was a huge wrench because the five years I had there have given me some fantastic memories.

'After all we went through as a team you cannot describe the elation when we won the Championship in 2003 – the memories I have from that season will stay with me forever, and the friends I made in Sussex I hope I will keep for life.'

Yasir Arafat (2006)

The four months he spent with Sussex in the second half of the 2006 season were the making of Yasir Arafat as a cricketer. He arrived in June as an unheralded replacement for Rana Naved, who was joining up with Pakistan for their tour of England, and finished it with two winners' medals, a three-year contract with Kent and a growing reputation, which was eventually to lead to international recognition back home the following year.

Arafat was not a total unknown when he arrived at Hove. He had played for Scotland in the one-day League for a couple of years when he was not professional, for the Clydesdale club in Glasgow, but if truth be told the only Yasir Arafat most Sussex supporters had heard of was the Palestinian political leader with not quite the same spelling! But Mushtaq Ahmed knew his compatriot had a latent talent which was still unfulfilled. He had worked with him in Pakistan's academy in Lahore during the off-season, and when Sussex began the task of finding a short-term replacement for Rana, Mushtaq wasted no time in recommending him to coach Mark Robinson. 'I will look after him,' promised Mushtaq, who was true to his word.

From the start, Sussex liked what they saw. Like Rana, Arafat was capable of swinging the new ball at good pace and, like any Pakistan fast bowler worth his salt, he could reverse-swing the old ball as well. And in the hot, dry summer of 2006 that was a potentially devastating skill, especially at Hove, where the square quickly turned a parched light brown.

With the bat, Arafat may have lacked Rana's explosive hitting ability, but he was far more adept at building an innings. On his debut at Arundel against Yorkshire he made a composed 86 and then took wickets with successive balls – including England captain Michael Vaughan – as Sussex cantered to an innings victory. He played in eight Championship games and finished with 41 wickets at 24.85, an impressive effort considering that in the second half of the season the bulk of the bowling was again done by Mushtaq. It included two five-wicket hauls. He also averaged an impressive 43.33 with the bat, and it was no surprise when several counties expressed an interest in signing him.

For the end-of-season game at Trent Bridge, Rana was available again and Sussex were obliged to pick him. But, typically, they invited Arafat along as part of the squad, and one of the abiding memories of the celebrations that accompanied a second Championship triumph was the sight of Mushtaq, Rana and Arafat cavorting together on the Trent Bridge outfield, toasting the success with nothing stronger than a diet cola. By then Arafat had agreed his Kent deal, and it was no surprise that he came back to haunt his former county in the third match of the 2007 season, when he took five wickets and scored a maiden Championship hundred on his home debut.

Tony Cottey

When Tony Cottey left Glamorgan in 1999, two years after helping the county to the Championship, he did so with a heavy heart. Nothing had given this proud Welshman more pleasure than representing his country – which is what the county feels like for every Glamorgan cricketer – and he could not imagine that playing for another county would instil the same sense of pride. He was wrong. And when Cottey brought the curtain down on his career in 2004, a year after he had joined an exclusive club of players who had won the Championship with two different counties, he was in tears.

His first four seasons with the club yielded modest returns for a player of his quality, and even at the start of 2003 he continued to struggle. When he was ruled out of a match at The Oval in

Young supporter Josh Poysden shows his allegiance during Tony Cottey's final game for the county in 2004.

The diminutive Tony Cottey batting in what was his final appearance for Sussex, against Surrey at Hove in 2004.

June through injury, and when his replacement Mike Yardy almost saved the game with a grafting half-century, Cottey firmly believed that he would end his career quietly in Sussex's second team. But Peter Moores kept faith. He was restored for the next game against Kent, to the astonishment of many Sussex supporters, and after making a first-innings duck he crafted his third half-century of the season in the second dig as Sussex claimed a crucial victory.

Frustratingly, it was his last innings for more than three weeks, because he did not take part in the Twenty20 Cup, but when Championship action resumed he played what was undoubtedly his finest innings for the county, 188 against Warwickshire. In the next match against Essex at Arundel he fell just two runs short of scoring a century in both innings and then made another hundred against Leicestershire. In total he scored nine half-centuries in 10 successive innings, one short of C.B. Fry's county record, which has stood since 1900, and finished the season with 1,149 runs. It earned him a one-year contract extension when his intention was to retire at the end of the 2003 season.

When Sussex signed Ian Ward in 2004, Cottey knew he would have to battle for his place, and he was left out at the start of the season and instead captained the second team. But he returned to the side to play nine more games and scored a match-winning 185 against Kent, the 31st and last first-class hundred of his 18-year career. Even when his form was deserting him, there was no one better for lifting morale in the dressing room.

'Whereas the common focus for our unity at Glamorgan was Wales, at Sussex it was far more the club and the traditions it stood for, and more than anything our anthem *Good Old Sussex by the Sea*,' he recalls in his engaging autobiography, which is being published in 2008.

'Due to the massive Welsh ties I had with Glamorgan, I didn't really believe I'd ever experience at Sussex the close-knit feeling I'd been central to at Glamorgan.

'Part of me felt that I'd never really fit in with these people from the heart of England's south, and as anyone who knows me well, Lord Ted Dexter I am not!

'However, in reality, at the end of my six years at Sussex I felt just as much of a wrench driving through the club gates at Hove for the last time as I did when I drove away from Sophia Gardens.'

Cottey still keeps in touch with a lot of his old Sussex teammates and is a welcome visitor to the dressing room when the county make their now infrequent visits to Wales. Business interests and after-dinner speaking keep him busy these days.

Mark Davis (2001–05)

It cannot have been easy playing in the shadow of Mushtaq Ahmed, but no one could underestimate the value of 'Davo's' contribution to Sussex's Championship success in 2003. Ask any of his teammates that year to name the performance which did more than any other to turn their dreams of glory into reality and, to a man, they will remember the career-best 168 he made against Middlesex, which helped achieve a precious victory from a seemingly hopeless position.

South African-born Davis had been the county's number-one spinner for the first two years of his Sussex career, but when Mushtaq arrived his opportunities became more

Off-spinner Mark Davis was part of the 2003 Championship-winning squad before embarking on a coaching career at Hove.

Mark Davis, one of the unsung heroes of the Sussex success story, appeals against Northamptonshire in 2003.

limited. But, at Hove in particular, Sussex always looked to play two slow bowlers, and Davis, who offered exemplary control, was often the perfect foil for Mushtaq. He was also an extremely capable lower-order batsman.

'Winning that Championship in 2003 was a very emotional moment and definitely the highlight of my career. The feeling when we won it and did a lap of honour around the ground will live with me forever,' he said. 'I didn't have a great season with the ball, but after that innings against Middlesex I felt I had made a contribution. When the side needed it most, I chipped in.'

Davis played in 13 more Championship games after 2003, but only four in 2005. By then he was taking on more coaching responsibility at the club, and the natural move when Peter Moores left at the end of 2005 to take charge of the England Academy was to give Davis the job of second-team coach, previously occupied by Moores's successor Mark Robinson.

It is a job he continues to do and in 2007 he was proud to coach the side that won the Second XI Championship – the first time Sussex had won the title since 1990.

Murray Goodwin (2000–present)
Mushtaq Ahmed has undoubtedly had the single biggest impact on Sussex's success since 2003, but Sussex would not have enjoyed an unprecedented period of achievement without the stellar contribution of Murray Goodwin. During the county's new golden age the 35-year-old Zimbabwean has been their most consistent batsman and, as he starts his eighth season at Hove, is still the Sussex wicket coveted

Murray Goodwin cuts loose against Lancashire at Hove in August 2002, his second season with Sussex.

above all others by opposition bowlers. The facts speak for themselves. Since his debut in 2001, Goodwin has been leading scorer every season apart from 2004 when Sussex had a soft landing in the year after winning their first Championship. As long as cricket is played in the county, he will be remembered for one thing above all else – the pull shot for four off Leicestershire's Phil DeFreitas at a packed County Ground on Thursday 18 September 2003, which secured the oldest first-class county their first Championship.

Goodwin took hundreds off some of the best attacks in the world during a career that earned him 19 Test caps and 71 one-day internationals for Zimbabwe, where he lived until he was 14 before he emigrated to Perth, Western Australia and which, for half the year at least, is now the place he calls home. But nothing could rival *that* moment as he fulfilled a pledge he had made to his teammates earlier in the day when he told them *he* would score the winning runs. Just for good measure, he went on to compile 335 not out, breaking the record for Sussex's highest individual score, which had stood since 1930.

Goodwin has been a mainstay of the Sussex middle order since 2002, but it is often forgotten that when he joined the county he opened the batting with Richard Montgomerie. That was only sprung on him when he was being driven to Hove from the airport, but Goodwin told Peter Moores he was happy to do anything to help the team. He made a pretty decent job of it as well, scoring 1,521 runs – a total which he has only bettered on one occasion since, in 2006. It included 203 against Nottinghamshire, which was then Goodwin's highest score, out of an unbroken stand of 372 with Montgomerie.

After seven seasons, opposition bowlers should have worked out a plan for Goodwin by now. But he still cuts and pulls with murderous intent and is the best player of spin in the side, although he admits that that is only because he enjoys

Murray Goodwin on his way to a match-saving hundred against Surrey in May 2007.

**A typically aggressive shot
by Murray Goodwin.**

pitting his wits against Mushtaq Ahmed so much in the nets. Of course Goodwin suffers the same peaks and troughs as any other batsmen, but since 2003 he has averaged a touch under 54 in the Championship with 19 centuries, four more than his nearest rival Chris Adams. Of current domestic players, only Mark Ramprakash has been more consistent during the decade, and Goodwin has not been short of offers from other counties when his contract is running down. Sussex supporters feared 2004 might be his last season when he only agreed a one-year deal, but the following year he was declassified as an overseas player and became Sussex's first Kolpak signing. His current contract expires at the end of 2008, and it is hard to believe he will not be offered a new one.

Goodwin is one of the quieter men in the dressing room, but what he says tends to be remembered. He is fiercely competitive and, in recent seasons in particular, has increasingly been used by the coaching staff in a mentoring role for the younger batsmen. Certainly no one in the side is held in higher regard, and all his teammates love batting with him because of the encouragement he offers and the calm authority he exudes.

Goodwin passed 1,000 runs for the sixth time last season but was not there when the title was secured again against Worcestershire, having flown back to Australia a few days earlier for a family funeral. He followed events at Hove on the internet and was raising a glass in celebration in the early hours of a Perth spring morning. All the time Goodwin is in their side, Sussex will have a chance of winning more silverware.

Andrew Hodd (2003 and 2005–present)

ANDREW Hodd was one of the unexpected heroes of Sussex's 2007 Championship success. He started the season as understudy to Matt Prior, but when Prior broke into the England Test team in May he got his chance, four years after his only previous first-class appearance for the county for whom he had played all his junior cricket. How he took it! Hodd played in 12 games as Sussex clinched back-to-back titles and, while his glovework was as neat and tidy under pressure as the coaching staff knew it would be, his batting was a revelation. He finished with 475 runs at 33.92, including a maiden Championship century when Sussex hammered Yorkshire by an innings in September. He might lack Prior's destructive powers, but on several occasions Hodd demonstrated an unflappable temperament and sound technique.

In hindsight, the innings that set him up and gave him the belief that he could score big runs had come against India in July. Although the tourists' batting was nowhere near full strength they fielded a strong bowling attack, but Hodd made an undefeated 106 after a few nervous moments when he was stuck on 99 for 13 deliveries. A first hundred is an important staging post in any young player's career, and Hodd went from strength to strength.

Hodd had come on to the staff in 2003 but found himself below both Prior and Tim Ambrose in the pecking order. Other counties were alerted and, although he was given no guarantees, a move to Surrey at least meant he had only one wicketkeeper-batsmen to rival. The trouble was that

Andrew Hodd took his chance in 2007 when Matt Prior was promoted to the England set-up.

Jonathan Batty, a former Surrey captain, has been as much a part of The Oval scene as the famous gas-holders, and when Hodd arrived in 2004 he quickly realised that only an injury to Batty would give him the opportunity he desperately craved. In two seasons with Surrey he played only two first-team games.

'I suppose I left thinking the grass was going to be greener at Surrey,' he said. 'But I ended up taking for granted what I'd grown up with at Sussex – the work ethic and professionalism of the squad and the management.'

By the end of the 2005 season he was totally fed up, but he kept in touch with events at Hove and his mood improved when he heard that Tim Ambrose, who had also become disillusioned at a lack of opportunity to keep wicket, was not going to sign a new contract. A few days after Ambrose signed for Warwickshire, Hodd was agreeing to return to Sussex, even though Surrey had offered him an improved two-year contract. It was a decision he has never regretted, even though in his first season back he continued to play understudy to Prior and appeared in just two Championship matches.

'After two years when I had gone stale at Surrey I had to get my game back to where it needed to be,' he said. 'I regard myself as a natural wicketkeeper, but I worked hard to improve my batting so that when the opportunity came I was ready to take it.'

Ironically, Hodd's first game was against his former county, and he made a composed 43. A week later at Worcester, he scored his maiden half-century for the county and was up and running. No one was more pleased with the success Prior enjoyed in the early stages of his Test career, and it came as a huge shock to Hodd when he lost his England place at the start of 2008, ironically to Ambrose. But Hodd has done enough to suggest that he, like Ambrose before him, has the game to hold down a place in both forms of the game purely as a batsman.

Paul Hutchison (2002–03)

Not many players have won Championships with two different counties, but the likeable left-armer Paul Hutchison did. That he never fulfilled the outstanding promise he showed early in his career, when he played for England A and took seven Pakistan wickets on his first-class debut, is a matter of regret both in his native Yorkshire and in Sussex. A succession of debilitating injuries meant he had only a peripheral role in Yorkshire's title triumph in 2001, and when Sussex approached him he felt a move to the South Coast would revive a career in danger of stagnating.

Peter Moores worked hard in 2002 to remodel his action, largely to prevent him from suffering further back trouble, and certainly left Sussex a better bowler than he had been when he arrived. But injuries, particularly shin-splints, continued to plague him. Moores encouraged his new signing to bowl a yard quicker. With hindsight, Hutchison feels that this may have accelerated his early exit from the game. He said: 'It was a shame that things didn't work out for me at Sussex. Their strategy at that time was to bowl the ball hard into the pitch, on the theory that it would start to crumble and become uneven by the end

Paul Hutchison had two unfulfilled years with Sussex when he struggled for fitness.

of the match and ideal for Mushtaq Ahmed. It worked really well: they went from strength to strength, and I still have the highest regard for Peter as a coach.'

In 2003 Hutchison played in only four Championship games, and in one of those – against Kent at Tunbridge Wells – he bowled just five overs before James Kirtley replaced him in the match after his release from the England squad. When Sussex strengthened their bowling attack by signing Mohammad Akram, Hutchison felt he would have more first-team opportunities elsewhere and joined Middlesex, his third county in four years. But he was never far from the treatment table at Lord's, and after playing just nine Championship games in two seasons he was released in 2005 and headed back north. 'I had loads more problems there, and by the end of that season my wife was pregnant and I knew my time was up,' he reflected.

When Sussex have visited Headingley in recent years, Hutchison has always taken the opportunity to catch up with his old teammates. In more reflective moments, he might wonder if it could have been him rather than Ryan Sidebottom – another southpaw and contemporary from his early days at Yorkshire – whose international career would flourish under Moores. Hutchison now works as clothing manager for Romida Sports, the Yorkshire-based cricket specialists, and plays league cricket for East Bierley under the captaincy of Gavin Hamilton, who made his Test debut alongside Chris Adams in South Africa in 1999 but, like Hutchison, failed to fulfill his undoubted potential.

Carl Hopkinson (2002–present)

Sussex born and bred, Hopkinson has been an integral part of the side which has won back-to-back Championships. And as his own game matures and improves, the greater his contribution to future successes will be. His breakthrough year came in 2006 when he played in all 16 games, forming a new opening partnership with Richard Montgomerie. A maiden Championship hundred eluded him – and continues to do so – but he made six fifties, many of them in trying circumstances when his efforts were perhaps not as appreciated as widely beyond the boundary as they were in the dressing room.

Sussex opted for Chris Nash in the opener's role the following year, and Hopkinson played in only seven games. Perhaps it would have been more had he converted 83 at Worcester in May into that coveted century, as he should have done.

No one epitomises the quiet determination that pervades the Sussex dressing room more than 'Hoppo', who adds further value to the side with his fielding, either in the covers or as a fearless silly point when Mushtaq Ahmed is casting his spell. He is certainly one player who did not want the 2007 season to end. In the final one-day game of the season against Nottinghamshire at Hove he made his first century for the county – a superb unbeaten 123 two days after his 26th birthday.

Time will tell whether it was his 'coming-of-age' moment, but the hardworking Hopkinson will do everything to make sure it is.

Carl Hopkinson played his part in Sussex's back-to-back Championship triumphs.

Carl Hopkinson was an ever-present in 2006 but found his Championship opportunities limited the following year.

Kevin Innes made history when he became the first 12th man to score a hundred, against Nottinghamshire at Horsham in May 2003.

Kevin Innes (2002–04)

A Championship-winners' medal and a unique place in the record books – 2003 was undoubtedly the high watermark of Kevin Innes's professional career.

Innes played in the same England Under-19 team as Michael Vaughan and Marcus Trescothick, but at the start of 2002 he was struggling to get into Northamptonshire's side. It was a difficult decision to make, especially as he had played for the county's second team at 14, but Innes decided to cut his ties with Wantage Road. Essex did not fancy him when he had a trial at Chelmsford, but within a month of arriving at Hove he was making his Championship debut for the county.

His big moment came the following May against Nottinghamshire at Horsham – the game which ignited Sussex's Championship challenge – when he became the first 12th man in history to score a hundred. James Kirtley, who had been left out of the England squad, was on his way to Cricketfield Road

Kevin Innes plays a sweep shot.

as Innes was compiling an unbeaten 103 that was his maiden first-class century. Shortly after reaching the milestone, he departed to a standing ovation and within minutes was attending to 12th-man duties in the dressing room, while reflecting on a moment he will never forget.

'If I could bottle the emotion I felt when I reached that hundred I would be a very rich man – it was the proudest day of my career,' he said.

Innes played in four more Championship games, but his second half of the season was badly affected by a groin injury. He played just twice in 2004 and was released at the end of the season. In 2005, Innes played against his former club when Sussex visited Luton to play Bedfordshire in the C&G Trophy – their most recent match against a minor county. He made just six and bowled four expensive overs for 39 runs as Sussex cantered to an eight-wicket win, but nevertheless Innes enjoyed catching up with old colleagues.

He is back at Northamptonshire these days, as performance manager for the county's youth squad.

James Kirtley steams in.

James Kirtley (1995–present)

A Sussex side without James Kirtley straining every sinew as leader of the bowling attack is hard to imagine, although, regrettably, it is one the county's supporters have had to get used to in the last couple of years, particularly in the Championship. Kirtley remodeled his action for the second time in his career in the winter of 2005–06, and although he remains a key component of Sussex's one-day side he has not made the contribution to the county's last two titles that he would have liked.

In 2006 he played in seven games and took 16 wickets, and the following year he only appeared in four matches and not at all after the meeting with Surrey at Hove in May. His solitary wicket was taken

James Kirtley has twice had to remodel his bowling action.

in the opening home fixture against Kent. No Sussex player in recent times has had to overcome as much adversity as Kirtley, the second-longest serving player on the staff behind Jason Lewry, and it would be foolish to write him off just yet, particularly as his performances in one-day cricket remain so consistently good. There is no better bowler in the crucial closing overs than Kirtley, and it was no surprise, given his form in 2007, that he earned an unexpected but thoroughly deserved recall to the England side for the inaugural Twenty20 World Cup.

Has Kirtley lost his potency since remodeling his action? The statistics would suggest so, but it is also worth remembering that, at 33, he is not going to be as fast as he was in his prime when he spearheaded the Sussex attack for so long. The highlight of his career was undoubtedly in 2003. In the late summer, his unstinting belief in his own ability was finally rewarded when he made his England Test debut against South Africa before helping his county win their first Championship a few weeks later.

'It was an amazing time,' he recalled. 'Everything I wanted to achieve happened in the space of a few weeks.'

Kirtley did not appear in any of Sussex's last five Championship games as he tried to establish himself in the England side before succumbing to shin-splints. But the ovation he received at Hove on the third day of the title-clinching game against Leicestershire was nearly as memorable as the moment the Championship had been secured the previous day. He finished one wicket short of claiming 50 in a season for the fifth year running.

Kirtley's best moments since have been in the one-day shirt, not least his Man-of-the-Match performance in the 2006 C&G Trophy Final against Lancashire. Off the field he has begun planning for the future by venturing into the cricket-clothing business with some success, so much so that MKK Sports had to move to enlarged premises in Eastbourne at the start of 2008 as his enterprise blossomed. It is hard to believe that the county will not make use of his vast experience in some capacity when he retires, perhaps as a bowling coach. But Kirtley still has something to offer on the pitch and a renaissance after two relatively lean years in first-class cricket should not be ruled out.

Jason Lewry (1994–present)

One day Sussex will start the season without the finest left-arm swing bowler English cricket has seen in the last

The evergreen Jason Lewry.

Jason Lewry was regarded by many as the best left-arm bowler in England until the emergence of Ryan Sidebottom in 2007.

few years – and that includes Ryan Sidebottom. It has become a Hove ritual – at the start of the season Lewry confesses that this might be his last year. By the end of it, having made a telling contribution to the Sussex success story, he commits himself for another season.

There is no doubt about it, Lewry has got better with age. Never the most self-confident of cricketers, perhaps he has learned to relax and truly enjoy himself in the last couple of years. Admittedly, the pre-season fitness work is more difficult than ever (and he never found it easy), and by the end of the season it can be a struggle just to lever himself out of bed in the morning, far less contemplate 20 overs on an unyielding Hove track. Lewry has made vital contributions to Sussex's last two Championship successes that have probably surprised him. In 2006 he took 57 wickets at 23.17, his best return since 1998, and he might have got close again a year later had it not been for the total washout at The Oval in August and a knee injury that kept him out of the last two matches. Nevertheless, only two Sussex bowlers took more than his 31 wickets at 30.09.

Lewry could only have dreamt of the career he has had when he joined Sussex in 1994 after terrorising club batsmen for Goring for years. He did not even have a proper run-up when he started, ambling in off four paces, but boy could he swing the cricket ball. Who knows what more he could have achieved had he possessed more self-belief and had a back operation not cruelly sidelined him in 1997 when the England selectors were starting to take notice. A solitary A tour seems scant reward for a player of Lewry's ability, when you consider some of the bowlers England have employed during the last 10 years.

Lewry was there in Sussex's dark days at the start of the Peter Moores era, so the success they finally enjoyed in 2003 meant as much to him as anyone. He took 41 wickets that season and would have finished with more had injury not sidelined him for five games. And there was a maiden first-class fifty as well, as anyone at Colchester who saw it will never forget.

So how long can he go on for? Sussex treat him carefully these days. He is rarely involved in one-day cricket (although you suspect he would like to have played more), and at 37 he needs to look after his body even more carefully. But Sussex are always a better side with him in it. As well as conventional swing, he has learned the art of reverse-swing in recent years, and when conditions allow there is still no more skillful exponent in the country. He admitted to a touch of envy when his old coach plucked Sidebottom from the county ranks in 2007 and made him into an established England cricketer. It could have been Lewry. Perhaps it should have been.

Chris Liddle (2007–present)

Sussex signed the left-arm pace bowler from Leicestershire at the end of 2006, and the 24-year-old's development was expected to be confined largely to second-team cricket in his debut season. In the event, he played in two Championship games, on both occasions when injuries badly affected the squad. He made a wicketless debut when Sussex were rolled over in less than seven sessions against Warwickshire at the end of April and had to wait until the title-clinching game at home to Worcestershire for his next appearance. Again he failed to take a wicket, although a good economy rate allowed Mushtaq Ahmed to attack from the other end, but he showed no little promise with the bat, coming in at number 10 to score his maiden half-century as Sussex took control of the match.

Liddle bowls out-swingers at a decent pace and uses his height (6ft 5in) to extract bounce. He spent the winter of 2007–08 in the indoor school, grooving his action under the watchful eye of coach Mark Robinson and working on the ball that moves into the batsmen. The indications were that he could have a greater role in Sussex's bid for a hat-trick of Championships.

Robin Martin-Jenkins (1995–present)

A number of players have threatened Martin-Jenkins's position as Sussex's leading all-rounder in recent years, but he has seen them off and played crucial roles in all of the county's triumphs since 2003, both in Championship and one-day cricket. Only four players have made more Championship appearances during that time, and although he has occasionally lost his place due to a lack of form with the bat, it is never long before he is back in the mix. Given his record, particularly in one-day cricket, it is something of a mystery why he has never earned England recognition. Many less talented players with much worse records have done so during his time. Perhaps he lacked that yard of pace which England

Robin Martin-Jenkins took some key wickets in all three Championship successes.

Robin Martin-Jenkins and Mushtaq Ahmed in animated discussion.

selectors seemed fixated with for so long. Not that Sussex ever complained. Martin-Jenkins gives his captain control, enabling Adams to attack at the other end through one of his strike bowlers or Mushtaq Ahmed. He had his best season with the ball since 2003 in 2007, when he took 30 Championship wickets at just 20.80 apiece. In Sussex's first title-winning season he claimed 31. Like most of their seam bowlers, his workload in recent years has decreased because of the number of overs bowled by Mushtaq, which means he can always give his all in short four or five-over bursts. He has always had a happy knack of getting good players out.

His form with the bat has been less consistent, but although the effects of a long summer were beginning to show at the end of season, his form was such that he did not want it to end. He scored 248 of his 428 runs in his last four innings and came agonizingly close to his first century since 2002, falling just one run short in the final game against Worcestershire. It was hard to say who felt more disappointed – RMJ or his father Christopher, who was covering his last county match as cricket correspondent of *The Times*.

'Tucker' remains a key member of Sussex's one-day side, and he shows no signs of giving way to younger rivals just yet. Having been involved with Sussex all of his cricket life, he will be a deserved beneficiary in 2008.

Richard Montgomerie (1999–2007)

The sound of Richard Montgomerie bashing the toe-end of his bat into the side of his right foot has become as synonymous with the County Ground as squawking seagulls and the wind blowing through the deckchairs. Not any more. Montgomerie led his teammates off for the last time after Sussex had completed the victory over Worcestershire that sealed the Championship, having announced his retirement from the game earlier in the day to take up a teaching appointment at Eton College.

It was not as difficult a decision as you might have imagined. Montgomerie has played county cricket since 1991, but he felt it was time to start the next part of his life, and to sign off having helped Sussex win a third title in five years – well, there could be no better way to finish.

'It has been an amazing nine years and an honour and a privilege to play for Sussex,' he said. 'There were some painful times at the start of my Sussex career, such as finishing bottom in 2000, but you have to go through the bad times to appreciate the success. Personally, the highlight was the first Championship, but all the trophies we have won have been so special.'

He departed with few regrets, except perhaps his lack of England recognition. 'I would love to have played for my country, but I knew three years ago that it wasn't going to happen,' he added. 'My motivation then was being part of a successful Sussex team.'

It remains to be seen just how much Sussex will miss Montgomerie's reassuring presence at the top of their batting order. He finished with a first-class average of 35.84 and scored 29 hundreds, 20 of them for Sussex and two in his final season. His one-day record was even better, boosted by two centuries in his final season, which gave him a career average of 37.54. Sussex have tried several opening partnerships during Montgomerie's time, but he has been a constant and familiar presence, missing only two Championship games since 2003. Sussex will also miss him for his close fielding. Mushtaq Ahmed would not have enjoyed his own spectacular success since 2003 had it not been for Montgomerie's bravery at 'boot hill'. He retired as the best short-leg fielder in the county game.

Never one to show much emotion, even Monty had a tear in his eye at the dinner to celebrate the success of 2007, when he was given a three-minute standing ovation. His right foot is probably glad he has retired at the age of 36, but he will be desperately missed at Hove.

Richard Montgomerie takes evasive action as Surrey's run-machine, Mark Ramprakash, goes on the attack at Hove in May 2007.

Chris Nash cemented his position at the top of the batting order in 2007.

Chris Nash (2002 and 2004–present) It is a question which might provoke much head-scratching among Sussex supporters in a few years' time. Which three players took part in every Championship game in 2007? Most fans would get Chris Adams and Mushtaq Ahmed, but perhaps not Chris Nash. The 25-year-old batsman from Horsham made his Championship debut while still at university in 2002 as an off-break bowler batting at number nine against Warwickshire. He took two wickets and was bowled for a golden duck.

By the start of 2007 he had only played twice more in the Championship, near the end of the previous season, and it was a minor surprise when Sussex opted for him instead of Carl Hopkinson as Richard Montgomerie's opening partner. A maiden hundred eluded him, but by the end of the summer he had done enough to justify Sussex's faith in him. He made seven fifties, but frustratingly, once the hard work had been done, concentration let him down and he would get out to a poor shot. The closest he came to a century was 89 in the title-clincher against Worcestershire when he put on 155 with Montgomerie, one of their three century partnerships.

Surely it is only a matter of time before he reaches that important milestone in every young player's career. What 2007 showed was that technically Nash is good enough to cope with the very best new-ball bowlers. He plays spin well, too, and made strides forward in one-day cricket as well, after an uncertain start. With Mushtaq Ahmed in the side, his opportunities to bowl are limited. But he was proud, if a little embarrassed, to finish top of the averages in 2007 with three wickets at 12.00, albeit from just 9.1 overs.

Congratulations from Matt Prior for Mark Robinson after he ran out Surrey's Ian Ward at Hove in May 2001.

Nash wintered in New Zealand in 2007–08 and began the new season determined to push on, even though it will be with a different opening partner following Montgomerie's retirement.

Matt Prior (2001–present)

Like Shakespeare's Banquo, Matt Prior must have felt like a ghost at the feast when Sussex clinched their third title in five seasons. The 25-year-old wicketkeeper-batsman played in the first three Championship games, making a highest score of 35, and briefly returned to the one-day side in June and for the Twenty20 Finals.

'It was a bit awkward at first being around the guys because I didn't really play much of a part in our success last year,' he said. 'But it didn't take long before the jokes and banter were flying again, and it was just great to be back in the Sussex dressing room.

'We had another fantastic season, and I don't think it's the end of the success either. Can we win three Championships in a row? Why not.'

While Sussex were pulling their season round after a terrible start, Prior was embarking on a rollercoaster few months with England. It began spectacularly with a century against the West Indies on his debut at Lord's, but by January 2008 he was out of the international picture altogether, dropped from the squads that toured New Zealand despite a batting average of 40.19 in his 10 Tests during 2007. Inconsistent glove-work, particularly on the tour to Sri Lanka, cost him his place, although there was general surprise that he was jettisoned altogether and widespread condemnation of the selectors in Sussex. Mark Robinson called the decision 'rubbish', and doubtless some of Prior's admirers would have used fruitier language than that.

For his part, Prior should feel no need to reproach himself over the contribution he made to Sussex's golden era – he has been an integral part of it. In the 2003 triumph his runs were crucial, particularly his three hundreds. It would have been easy for him to retreat into an introspective shell after losing the gloves to Tim Ambrose, but he responded with the sort of spirited performances that epitomised the county's first ever Championship success.

By the time of the next one in 2006 he had seen off his rival Ambrose and was established as the first-choice wicketkeeper-batsman. He had also played some one-day internationals, having enjoyed his first call-up in 2004, but increasingly consistent performances that season seemed to convince the selectors that he was the answer to England's perennial problem behind the stumps at Test level too. In 2006 Prior scored three hundreds and would have reached 1,000 runs had he not missed two games because of England one-day commitments. His keeping had also improved through his own determination to succeed and the work he did with his cricketing hero and now agent, Alec Stewart.

Peter Moores knows Prior's game better than anyone. They first worked together in the Sussex youth set-up when Prior was 12, and although Moores was taking something of a risk when he chose Prior in his first squad after becoming England coach it paid off spectacularly when Prior smashed an unbeaten 126 at headquarters and looked as if he was playing in his 50th Test match, not his first.

Matt Prior shows typical athleticism.

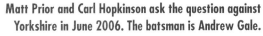

Matt Prior and Carl Hopkinson ask the question against Yorkshire in June 2006. The batsman is Andrew Gale.

Matt Prior on the attack.

The scenes at Hove that afternoon, when Sussex were mounting a rearguard action against Surrey, were almost as surreal as those on the last day of the season. It was often said of Ian Botham during his prime that he could empty the bars. That chilly Friday, Prior succeeded in filling them as Sussex supporters crowded around the pavilion TV sets to watch their man become the first England wicketkeeper to score a hundred on his Test debut. Conveniently, the umpires at Hove brought the teams off for bad light just as Prior reached the nineties. Brian Smith, who operates the gate at the bottom of the dressing-room steps, seemed in an unusual hurry to usher the players off the field when conditions got too gloomy. No wonder. He speaks most days to Prior and has never been short of an encouraging word, especially during Prior's formative years at Hove. No one could have been prouder of what he achieved than Prior himself.

Whatever has happened subsequently, that was a day Prior will never forget. He began 2008 back in the Sussex side, quietly determined to help his county fulfill his own prophecy at the end of last season by winning more silverware, while proving to the England selectors that they acted with undue haste when they dropped him.

Rana Naved (2005–07)

During the second day of their penultimate match of the 2007 season against Durham, Rana Naved badly dislocated his shoulder attempting a typically committed diving stop on the boundary's edge. As a stricken Rana lay motionless on the Riverside outfield, surrounded by his teammates, there were genuine fears that he had suffered a career-threatening injury. Play was suspended for 35 minutes and two ambulances were needed. It was hardly the way he wanted to end his Sussex career. Thankfully, the prognosis in hospital was more reassuring, but it was only a month before the start of the 2008 season that Rana was able to give his new county, Yorkshire, assurances that he was fit enough to join them as their overseas player.

Of course, the 29-year-old would still be at Hove had it not been for the ECB's contentious decision

Rana Naved in full flight.

to reduce the number of overseas players to one per county. It seems it is fine that the domestic game can be flooded with Kolpak imports, but not the star names which put bums on seats and excite county supporters. Rana certainly did that. The sight of him charging down the Hove slope and bowling his devastating mixture of in-duckers, out-swingers, yorkers and slower balls made him almost as popular during his time with the county as his more fêted Pakistan compatriot.

Peter Moores signed Rana on the recommendation of Mushtaq from what he had seen with his own eyes during Rana's first Test tour in the winter of 2005 to Australia. Pakistan lost the series 3–0, but in the final Test in Sydney, Moores noted Rana's willingness to bowl long spells and his ability to reverse-swing a ball that was only 35–40 overs old. He did not arrive at Sussex until mid-June, but soon made up for lost time with 54 wickets in just nine Championship appearances, his wickets costing just 19.92 runs apiece. He could bat as well and at Lord's scored 139 in a stand of 228 for the seventh wicket with Mike Yardy as Sussex scored 522 – the highest first-day total in the Championship for 20 years – and then bowled Middlesex out twice in a day, Rana finishing with seven wickets.

He performed even better in 2006, despite playing in only six Championship games before he suffered a groin injury against Middlesex at Horsham, which was to badly affect his participation in Pakistan's tour of England that summer. He took 35 Championship wickets at 16.72 apiece, including 11–148 at Headingley, the best match figures by a Sussex bowler against Yorkshire since 1907. In 2001 Rana had a trial with Yorkshire, but the county did not consider him good enough. It would take them seven years to see the error of their ways. Rana returned in 2007, fully fit and refreshed, and in 14 games he took 50 wickets, including two five-wicket hauls. And he again proved to be a key member of the one-day side as well.

There was always going to be a scramble for his signature when it was confirmed that Mushtaq would be staying as overseas player, with several counties interested. A humble but proud cricketer, Rana embraced the unique dressing-room atmosphere at Hove as much as any player. And if he did not already know the esteem with which Sussex supporters regarded him, the long line of them wishing to shake his one good hand during the title-clincher against Worcestershire would have shown him.

Ollie Rayner (2006–present)

Ollie Rayner is not the first German-born off-spinner to play for Sussex, but if he forges as successful a career as the other one – John Barclay – neither he nor the county will be complaining. Time will tell whether Rayner can emulate 'Trout', but the start of his career was certainly *Boys Own* stuff. Against the touring Sri Lankans in May 2006 – his first year on the staff – the 22-year-old from Eastbourne became the first Sussex batsman to score a century on his first-class debut, admitting afterwards that a tea-time pep talk from Sri Lanka's Test veteran Kumar Sangakarra had helped settle him down when he was in sight of the landmark.

The team management were always aware of Rayner's ability with the bat but were surprised,

Off-spinner Ollie Rayner was part of the successful side of 2007.

perhaps, by the temperament he showed that day. Mark Robinson had read him the riot act at the start of the year in terms of his general attitude, and the penny seemed to have dropped. At 6ft 5in, Rayner is always going to get bounce, and he turns the ball sharply. When Mushtaq Ahmed missed his first Championship game since joining the county a few weeks later, Rayner took three second-innings wickets against Kent and again impressed.

With Mushtaq omnipresent in the side and Saqlain Mushtaq recruited as well, Rayner had to bide his time last season and did not play in the Championship. He also played only six times in one-day cricket. But he continues to develop, and with Saqlain back at The Oval, he will be desperate to establish himself as second-choice spinner in 2008, despite the competition from Tom Smith and Will Beer.

Saqlain Mushtaq (2007)

A few days after the Championship was secured, Sussex announced that Saqlain Mushtaq had been released from his contract, which had a year to run, for family reasons. The Pakistan off-spinner had rebuilt his career at Hove after it had been threatened by injury and Sussex were hoping his rehabilitation would continue in 2008. Instead he is back at Surrey, where he had eight successful seasons, after expressing a wish to return to London.

When they signed the 31-year-old, Sussex knew that it would be a while before his fitness levels were sufficiently good enough for him to play a full part in the first team. It was a surprise when he was brought in for the hurly-burly of the Twenty20 Cup, and Chris Adams had to hide him in the field, but with the ball in his hand he showed that star quality which had brought him 208 Test wickets before his knees gave way.

Saqlain played just three games in the title-winning campaign, but still took 14 wickets at fewer than

Saqlain Mushtaq made some crucial contributions in 2007 before signing for Surrey.

20 runs each, including a five-for on his debut against Warwickshire. He also made an unbeaten half-century in the win over Yorkshire and relished playing competitively again, particularly with two compatriots, Mushtaq Ahmed and Rana Naved, alongside him.

On occasion, spectators and teammates would wince as he hobbled painfully after the ball at the end of a long day in the field, and it is clear that he can never expect to regain the mobility he once had, despite two major operations. However, during his one season on the South Coast, he proved beyond doubt that he is still a quality performer and that he can still bowl the 'doosra' – the delivery he invented nearly more than a decade ago.

Billy Taylor (1999–2003)

Only Billy Taylor himself can say whether he regrets leaving Sussex a few weeks after he helped them win their first Championship. It made sense to move when his native Hampshire came calling, but Taylor has not made the impact he would have liked, particularly in Championship cricket. He was a regular for the first season and a half, but since July 2006 has played just six Championship games and was restricted to seven one-day appearances last season. There was even speculation that Sussex might be interested in bringing him back to Hove.

Taylor's off-the-field activities seem to have created just as much interest in recent years. He trained as a tree surgeon and in the winter of 2007–08 has been working at a falconry centre in the New Forest, rekindling an interest he had as a teenager. He joined Sussex in 1999 after impressing in a trial match and played an integral part in helping the county achieve top-flight status in 2001, although he seemed permanently to be operating in the shadow of James Kirtley and Jason Lewry.

Two years later he appeared in seven Championship games in the title-winning campaign and took

21 wickets, 19 of them when James Kirtley was playing for England, and he had five games at the end of the season. His finest hour, perhaps even in his whole career, came in the crucial win over Lancashire in late August. The visitors were comfortably saving the game on the last afternoon when Taylor took four wickets in a marathon 17-over spell down the Hove slope. It was a performance that typified Taylor's wholehearted approach and one of no little skill, either. Taylor could swing the ball both ways and often did a containing job, which was appreciated more by his teammates than by those on

Billy Taylor played a key role towards the end of the season when Sussex clinched their first title in 2003.

All-rounder Luke Wright celebrates a wicket against Surrey in May 2007.

the other side of the boundary.

'It was disappointing that I was never considered one of the main bowlers at Hove,' he said at the end of the season. 'But I left Sussex a Championship winner, which was a massive achievement, and I think the supporters and members always appreciated that I did my best.'

Luke Wright (2005–present)

The role Luke Wright has in Sussex's bid for a hat-trick of Championships will be one of the intriguing sub-plots of the 2008 season. After signing a new three-year contract at the start of the year, Wright expressed his desire to bat higher up the order than number 8 and bowl more overs. In short, Wright wants to produce the sort of impact he made in one-day cricket in 2007 when his performances as a big-hitting opening bat, particularly in the Twenty20 Cup, propelled him into the England one-day set-up.

Perhaps he will get his wish, although while Mushtaq Ahmed is still in the side it is always going to be hard for any third or fourth-choice seamer. What Wright has shown is that he is capable of bowling short, high-energy spells of four or five overs, at decent pace, which can unsettle even well-set batsmen and which, more often than not, get his captain a vital breakthrough.

In one-day cricket he made two outstanding hundreds in 2007, and in the Championship he showed he could get his head down when the situation demanded it by scoring three half-centuries. The pick of them came against Hampshire at Arundel when he made 57 and helped the last two first-innings wickets add 108 runs and tilt the balance of the match Sussex's way.

Wright made his Championship debut for Leicestershire in the match in which Sussex clinched the title in 2003. None of the visiting bowlers was spared during those three days, but Peter Moores saw enough in Wright to suggest that 'he had something about him.' He returned to Hove the following April a Sussex player, and although his career was not progressing at the rate Wright would have hoped, all that changed in 2007.

Sussex gave him his head in the Twenty20 Cup at the top of the order, and their faith was repaid in spectacular style. He finished the domestic competition as leading run-scorer and a few weeks later was facing some of the best bowling attacks in the world in the inaugural Twenty20 World Cup. To prove his domestic success was not a fluke, he scored a polished half-century on his debut in the one-day international against India in September.

That, and an injury caused when he slipped on a wet outfield at the Rose Bowl and missed the visit

Luke Wright's explosive ability with bat and ball earned him England recognition in 2007.

to Lancashire, meant Wright played only a peripheral part as Sussex closed in on their third title in five years. He made just two appearances in the second half of the season and was passing through an Indian airport, en route from Johannesburg to Sri Lanka for a one-day series, when he heard that Sussex were champions again.

Playing for his country has infused this naturally confident cricketer with even more self belief, which he is desperate to translate into more match-winning performances in the Championship side.

He said: 'The captain and coach want me to have more responsibility in 2008, which was great to hear. My performances in one-day cricket have got me into the England side, which is fantastic, but Test cricket is the ultimate ambition for every player, and I'm no different, and that means playing an even bigger role in four-day cricket.'

Mike Yardy (2000–present)

It took four seasons for Mike Yardy to confirm what sound judges at Hove, most notably Peter Moores, knew all along – the boy could play. For the first three years of his career he was regarded as a rather stodgy player, someone who could never be accused of lacking spirit or fight and who never surrendered his wicket. He was restricted to just two Championship appearances in Sussex's first title-winning season, the most memorable a valiant vigil of more than five hours, which almost earned Sussex

Mike Yardy opens his shoulders against Surrey at the Oval in 2005.

a draw against Surrey before he was last man out with just 5.2 overs to survive. He made a stylish 47 later in the season in a rain-affected draw against Nottinghamshire and while, as a Sussex boy, Yardy relished the celebrations at the end of the season as much as anyone, he was acutely aware that he needed to make improvements to his own game if he were to have a future with the county.

The following winter he did just that – in between shifts working at a sports shop at Gatwick Airport – but it was not until the final match of 2004 that he truly arrived on the Sussex scene with a maiden hundred against Surrey. He started the following season with another century against the same opponents and embarked on a run of form which took him to the top of the domestic batting averages, his zenith coming against the Bangladeshis when he made 257 – the highest score by a Sussex batsman against a touring team. Just for good measure, he also took 5–83 with his under-rated left-arm spin, another career best. He scored three more Championship centuries and finished the season with 1,217 runs at 48.68. Only the imperious Murray Goodwin – a player Yardy admires more than anyone else at Hove – finished above him in the averages.

Yardy did even better in the Championship-winning season a year later, with three hundreds and an average of 50.77. He would have passed 1,000 runs again had he not been called into the England one-day squad in August, although he did return for the title-clincher against Nottinghamshire. He made his England debut two days after helping Sussex win the C&G Trophy and spent the following winter shadowing the Ashes party as part of the England Development squad.

However, Yardy has lived through enough of the bad times to know that, just when everything appears to be going to plan, it can quickly go wrong. For him, that moment arrived at Lord's in April 2007, when his finger was shattered by a delivery from Steve Harmison during the annual pre-season game between the champion county and MCC. To add insult to injury Yardy was on 99 at the time. He missed the first two months of the season as a result, and when he did return to the side he was soon out of it again on England one-day duty. He played in 10 games and scored one hundred against Yorkshire.

'We won the Championship again, which was fantastic, but from a personal point of view it was a poor season compared to the previous two,' he said.

'But by the end of it I had got my head right again. I was worrying about too many things, and I had to free my mind to concentrate on the basics which, for me, is just about scoring runs. That's what gives me the most pleasure in cricket.'

After three hectic winters with England, a few weeks away from the game with his young family also helped, and by the time the Lions set off for their tour of India in January this year Yardy was refreshed and ready for the next stage of his career.

Chapter 5
The Longest Wait

EVEN Father Time must have dozed off, dropping his scythe and hourglass, as he waited for Sussex to win the County Cricket Championship. The oldest of the first-class counties was formed in 1839, and 164 years passed before the famous winning of the domestic game's blue riband; that is two long lifetimes placed end to end. Waiting for Godot was easier than this.

Some said that Sussex's ultimate triumph in 2003 was all the sweeter for its elusiveness. Well, it may have been – for the living. And even they had to show the patience of Penelope, who weaved and unravelled on each faithful day as she waited for her husband, Odysseus, to return from the Trojan war. Then, having enjoyed their historic success, Sussex decided to do it again. They won it in 2006 and, by way of a reprise, in 2007 as well. So the long-suffering supporters who, consulting watches and timetables, had paced up and down outside Hove BN3 3AN for more than a century and a half as they waited for an open-top bus to come along, looked on, bewildered, as three arrived at almost the same time.

Until captain Chris Adams and coach Peter Moores ushered the club into the richest epoch in its long and exotic history, supporters had to content themselves with the dubious glory of second place. There is, after all, a thwarted heroism, a sort of noble stoicism, about coming second. At least, that is how some beleaguered members consoled themselves. At least runners-up often sweat more than winners who, more talented or more experienced, can appear to work less hard for the spoils. You can see 'if only!' etched in the desperate features of the second-placed, that forlornness in the eyes that identifies the best of the rest. Sussex cricketers, it seemed, were born not with silver spoons in their mouths, but silver medals round their necks.

The county's supporters, one imagines, had little time for Amundsen. For most, the tragic Scott of the Antarctic has the greater, the more enduring, appeal. Pete Sampras, seven times a Wimbledon winner, was one of the greatest tennis players who ever lived. But was he really more heroic than Ivan Lendl or Ken Rosewall, who were obsessed with winning on the famous lawns and reached six Finals between them, only to trudge away weary and defeated on each occasion? Stephen Hendry, similarly, is perhaps the greatest snooker player the game has seen, winning seven world titles. But it is Jimmy White, who has reached six Finals and been beaten in all of them, whose heart-aching failures are seared on the memory.

It was by these doubtful means, with rueful shrugs and cheerful resignation, that the supporters of Sussex County Cricket Club sustained themselves until they finally won the County Championship five years ago. Before that, they had been runners-up on seven occasions, seven bridesmaids for seven summers. Now only Somerset, Northamptonshire, Gloucestershire and the new boys at Durham have failed to lift domestic cricket's greatest prize. And Durham came close in 2007 – runners-up for the first time. Arguably, Sussex won the title in 1875, when they finished joint top with Nottinghamshire and Lancashire, but the competition was only formally recognized in 1890, and today the fight for recognition for that summer 133 years ago seems to have lost some of its urgency. Real prizes have been seized, and there is no longer the need to scuffle for hoary trifles.

This is the third Golden Age of Sussex cricket. The first came in English cricket's Golden Age, the late Victorian and Edwardian period before World War One, when Britain still ruled the world's waves and cricket fields. This was the Sussex of, above all, C.B. Fry and Ranjitsinhji, the best two batsmen in England at the turn of the century. But there was also Fred Tate, Joe Vine, Albert Relf and George Cox senior. The second great epoch came in the early 1930s, when they were second for three successive seasons under three different captains. This Sussex side boasted such names as Duleepsinhji, Maurice Tate, John and James Langridge, Jim and Harry Parks and Ted Bowley. They were runners-up in 1932, 1933 and 1934.

Sussex then had to wait until 1953 before they came second once more under the inspirational leadership of David Sheppard. They should never have challenged mighty Surrey, but they did, thanks to young Jim Parks, Ian Thomson, Ken Suttle and – yes, again – John and James Langridge. Their seventh second came in Ian Botham's *annus mirabilis* of 1981, when an old Etonian called John Barclay brought together the disparate talents of Imran Khan, Garth le Roux, Gehan Mendis, Paul Parker, Geoff Arnold and Ian Gould. They were probably the best side that year, although Nottinghamshire supporters might have different memories. But this is the greatest of all ages for Sussex cricket. This time the gold has the patina, the sheen of the real thing. The jeweller has his eyepiece in and is nodding vigorously. Suddenly those periods early in the 20th century and again 30 years later look like so much fool's gold.

Until recent times, the county was much more adept at finishing at the other end of the table. They have ended up bottom of the Championship on 10 occasions since 1890, when there was even talk of having their first-class status withdrawn. Unofficially, they also finished sucking the wooden spoon in 1877, 1878, 1882, 1883, 1885, 1888 and 1889, the club's 50th birthday. They have been bottom six times since 1968 and as recently as 1987, 1990, 1997 and 2000. The long wait for prizes goes back much further than 1839, because the history of cricket in Sussex is as old as the game itself.

The first recorded match in the county was played at Sidlesham back in 1611. But at least there was the occasional glory of beating an England XI, whom they played regularly between 1827 and the middle of the 19th century. The first great Sussex side, in Championship terms, started to come together in the 1890s. The imperious Fry arrived in 1894 and was followed, next year, by the silk-clad Kumar Shri Ranjitsinhji – or Smith, to his mates at Cambridge. He scored 1,766 runs at an average of 50.16, with four hundreds, in that first summer with the county in all Sussex matches.

Sussex were ninth in 1898, when Ranji spent the summer in India attending to various royal duties, but, when he returned the following year they jumped to fifth. They were third in 1900 and fourth in

1901 when Ranji and Fry enjoyed a vintage season together. 'For three or four years Sussex were the best batting side in England,' said Sammy Woods, the great Somerset all-rounder. 'More people went to see Sussex than any other side.' Then, in 1902, the county embarked on their frustrating sequence of seconds. It was a famous season. An Ashes summer. And very wet. It was made famous by Victor Trumper and Gilbert Jessop, by Bill Lockwood, Wilf Rhodes, George Hirst, Clem Hill and Hugh Trumble. Jessop scored an astonishing hundred in 75 minutes, before, famously, Rhodes and George Hirst saw England home at The Oval. The series had already been lost, but this match, coming at a time when the nation was still coming to terms with the death of Queen Victoria and the South African war, at least lifted the spirits of some.

Domestically, Yorkshire won their third title in as many summers. But after building up momentum in the previous seasons Sussex had felt that this might be their chance. According to the *County Annual* the team in 1902 was more than just Ranji and Fry.

'No longer are we dependent upon a couple of individuals but the whole team seemed to rise to the occasion, in a body, and the success of Sussex in 1902 was attributed to this cause. K.S. Ranjitsinhji, C.B. Fry, G. Brann, W. Newham, C.L.A. Smith, Tate, Vine, Relf, Killick, Butt and Cox all performed to perfection during the past season and it only remains for the county to advance another step in order to attain the desired haven – that of champion county.'

These, then, were the first of the nearly men. Note that the amateurs retained their initials – and bagged most of the best batting places. But despite the success of the summer there was little harmony in the dressing room. Ranji, the captain, again topped the batting averages with a Championship average of 66.61 but, according to the *Annual*, 'Considering that he only took part in a dozen matches, and that 667 of his 885 runs were obtained in four innings, it is evident that he cannot be looked upon with that certainty that characterised his previous seasons.

'Why he abandoned the team, with which he had been so closely connected, at the most critical stage of their programme it is not pleasant to dwell upon here, but we are happy to be able to record that a reconciliation has since taken place, and that the famous batsman will once again lead the Southern representatives during the coming season.'

In his splendid booklet, *Sussex – Seven Times the Bridesmaid*, Nicholas Sharp points to correspondence between Ranji and Billy Newham, who also served as the club's secretary between 1889 and 1908, and then assistant secretary until his death in 1944. Newham wanted Ranji to play on the club's western tour against Gloucestershire at Bristol and Somerset at Taunton. Ranji replied: 'There is a monstrously selfish spirit prevalent in the team...some of them are getting distinctly above themselves.'

Ranji did not appear on the tour, but did appear for the MCC against Australia at Lord's in August. In its report of the match at Taunton, *Cricket* Magazine said: 'Again deserted by C.B. Fry and Ranjitsinhji, who were for the second time in the week taking a rest, and moreover, obliged to do without Fred Tate, who was suffering from rheumatism, Sussex did very well indeed to avoid defeat.'

At the end of the season, Ranji made what appeared to be a peace offering when he invited four Sussex professionals to join him for a week's fishing and shooting in Yorkshire.

The main reason why Sussex went so close in 1902 was the bowling of Fred Tate, father of the legendary Maurice, who had the best season of his career, taking 161 wickets at 14.92 apiece, including figures of 15–68 against Middlesex. Some 153 of those wickets came in 20 Championship matches, and Albert Relf (56 wickets) came next. It is a sad irony that 'Chub' Tate, who bowled off-breaks at just under medium pace, usually in marathon spells, is best remembered for a famous dropped catch.

Particularly effective on damp pitches, Tate played his solitary Test match that summer, making his England debut against Australia at Old Trafford on his 35th birthday. Archie McLaren, the England captain, moved Tate from his customary position in the slips to the leg-side boundary. Joe Darling immediately skied the ball to him and the ball was grassed, a crucial miss in a low-scoring game.

Then Tate came to the wicket with England 116–9, needing 124 to win and level the series. There was a whiff of redemption in the air. But Tate was bowled for four, and England lost the match by three runs. Prophetically, Tate told his friend Len Braund, who had been bowling when he dropped the catch: 'I've got a little kid at home who'll make up for it to me.'

The following season was also exceptionally wet and with better luck Sussex, instead of Middlesex, might have won the title. Only one day's play was possible in both Middlesex games. Sussex were second once more in 1903. Remarkably, for such a sodden summer, Fry scored 2,446 runs and topped the county's and the country's batting averages. He scored eight centuries, including two in the match against Kent at Hove. Not even Ranji could match Fry's heavy scoring that year – he was second, with 1,394 runs at 58 – while Relf topped the bowling with 108 wickets at 19.09 apiece.

Despite the ultimate success of Middlesex, Yorkshire were still regarded as the best team in the land and very much the side to beat. Sussex did so twice and not without style. At Bradford, Sussex piled up 558–5, with Fry scoring 234 and Ranji 93. They won by an innings and 180 runs. Sussex won the low-scoring return at Hove by four wickets. This time the bowlers were the heroes, with Tate and Cox returning match figures of 10–75 and 9–83 respectively. Repeatedly, Sussex dominated matches only to run out of time because of the atrocious weather. They totally outplayed a powerful Surrey side, both at Hove, where they scored 542–9 (Fry 200), and at The Oval, where they made 600–7 (Ranji 204, Vine 104). But both matches were drawn after they had declared.

Sussex would not come so close to the Championship for almost three decades, but they remained a good side. They were sixth in 1904 when neither the weather nor the toss was on their side. Fry was so unlucky in the latter respect that he delegated responsibility to other players. Sussex remained unbeaten at home but failed to win a single match away. Ranji, who scored 99 and 207 not out against Lancashire without giving a chance, was back on top of the averages with 83.77. Five different amateurs led the side in 1905, when they were back up to third, but in many senses this was the year of the professional. Cox took 164 wickets, then a record for the county, while Relf and Ernest Killick achieved the double.

Sussex did not get close to winning the Championship in the 1920s, even though Maurice Tate and his county captain, Arthur Gilligan, opened the bowling for England on occasions and in 1924 bowled out South Africa for 30. These two catapulted Sussex to the top of the table and even took 76 wickets between them in a fortnight. But Gilligan was struck a heavy blow above the heart while batting in the Gentlemen versus Players match and would never bowl fast again. Gilligan and Tate, though, are the most famous pairing in Sussex cricket after Fry and Ranji. Tate was the greatest of Sussex's home-grown players. He scored 22,004 runs, including 21 centuries, with an average of 25.32, and took 2,784 wickets at 18.12 each. He reached his peak in the middle of the 1920s, taking more than 200 wickets a season between 1923–25. He was past his best, but still an important member of a very good side, when they came second for the third time in 1932.

Sussex came second in three successive summers as they did their best to dispel the notion that this was the Depression. It was a totally different side from 1903, but once again they had an Indian prince to inspire them. Duleepsinhji was Ranji's nephew and had the skill and artistry, if not the physical health, to rival his uncle. Here was a player good enough to score 333 in a day against Northamptonshire at Hove in 1930. In the same summer he scored a magnificent 173 for England against Australia in the second Test at Lord's. When he was out, caught at long-off trying to force the pace, the hard-to-please Ranji, gnawing an umbrella in the pavilion, was heard to mutter: 'The boy was always careless.'

Duleep captained Sussex in 1932, sadly his last season. He was a fine captain, and he said at the start of the season that with one more bowler the Championship could be won. But that extra bowler, like the last piece of the jigsaw that has been swallowed by the cat or fallen down the back of the sofa,

was never found. Their match against Yorkshire, the reigning champions, at Hove, was billed as the Championship decider and attracted a huge crowd. But Sussex lost, in their only defeat of the season. Anyone looking for excuses could find plenty. Duleep was taken ill and announced that he would not play again that season. He missed the final five matches because of tuberculosis and would never play for the county again. Bowley and Bert Wensley, the first good enough to open the batting for England, the second a fine all-rounder despite being overshadowed by Tate, were injured, and six of the team that did shuffle out to play were less than fully fit. They were bowled out for 166 and 150. Sussex were at their

'Young' Jim Parks.

family best this year, with John and James Langridge and Jim and Harry Parks, in addition to Duleep and Tate, who still managed to take 124 wickets. And their deep batting meant they had the tail of a Manx cat. But they could hardly complain when Yorkshire retained their title, winning 19 matches to Sussex's 14.

In 1933, even without the inspirational Duleep, they fared even better, winning more matches (18) than they had ever managed before.

'It was a glorious record,' wrote John Marshall in *Sussex Cricket: A History*, the definitive volume on the club.

'Mighty Yorkshire were substantially beaten twice – a feat no other county was able to emulate – and Sussex lost only two matches in a programme heavier than ever before, every county being played. Ten of the 18 wins were by an innings and Sussex averaged 10 runs per wicket more than their opponents.

'The Sussex season of 1933 will always be remembered for that mighty partnership of 490 by Bowley and John Langridge in 350 minutes in a single day against Middlesex at Hove.'

Sussex did the double over not only Yorkshire, but also Derbyshire, Gloucestershire, Northamptonshire, Somerset and Worcestershire, and were beaten just twice in the season. Jim Langridge was the first player in England to achieve the double that year and toured India in the winter. Tommy Cook was the side's most successful batsman, with 1,795 runs, including five centuries. Cook also played football for Brighton and Hove Albion and for England, even though he was a Third Division player. His batting was almost good enough to make him a double international. He was more than just a sportsman. He fought in both World Wars, first in the Royal Navy, where he was decorated, and then in the South African Air Force, where he was seriously injured. Tragically, separated from his wife and suffering depression, he killed himself a month before his 49th birthday in 1950.

If Sussex had looked good in 1932 and 1933 they looked even better as they pursued the elusive prize in 1934. The South African Oxford University skipper Alan Melville, had taken over the captaincy from R.S.G. Scott and led from the front, with three stylish centuries. Sussex led the table until the middle of August as Yorkshire faltered. Tate, in his 40th year, was still a force, taking 137 Championship wickets at 19, and he proved a thoughtful captain when called on to deputise. Jim Parks and Wensley were also effective all-rounders. Cook had an even better season, with 2,072 runs at an average of 56, and five others topped 1,000 runs, the Parks and Langridge brothers and Melville. The side once topped 500 and reached 400 on 11 occasions. So just how did they miss out on the title? A major reason was the decline of Jim Langridge as a left-arm spinner. He collapsed almost as dramatically as Devon Loch in the run-in at Aintree.

John Marshall again: 'A variety of reasons can be cited for the eventual failure, such as illness, accidents and the unenterprising batting. Above all there was the disastrous loss of form of that mainstay of Sussex cricket – and the side's only first-class slow bowler – over so many years, James Langridge. Success ebbed sadly away as the end of the season approached.

'He had a wonderful game against Yorkshire, taking 9–49, which helped materially towards the victory which gave Sussex the distinction of being the only county to beat Yorkshire thrice running between the wars.

'But after that an extraordinary and depressing thing happened to him. He lost his length and, moreover, was often no-balled. He finished seventh in the bowling averages with 48 wickets costing 28.35 runs each, compared with 136 at 15 each in the previous year.

'Happily this harrowing experience did not demoralise him and in subsequent seasons he became his old, accurate, dependable self again.'

But it was over for Sussex that year. Like Lancashire, they played 30 matches. Sussex won 12 and Lancashire, the champions, 13. It was the end of the nearly-men's most consistent challenge to date. In 1935 they fell back to seventh, and the following year they were back with the dead men in 14th. They would not get so close to the Championship again until a long world war had been fought, atom bombs had been dropped and the Welfare State had been created.

Jump from the 1930s to the 1950s, from Fred Astaire to Elvis. Okay, it was a young Elvis, but he was well on the way to stardom when Sussex came second for the sixth time in 1953. A queen was crowned, and Sir Edmund Hillary and Sherpa Tensing shinned up a famous peak. But winning the Championship was once again a summit beyond Sussex. There was, however, a great improvement on recent form. In the five seasons 1948–52 Sussex had finished 16th, 13th, 13th, 10th and 13th. Now, under the invigorating leadership of Sheppard, they were suddenly second and even managed to give Surrey, with one of the most dominating sides in Championship history, a run for their money.

Sheppard had been a relatively ordinary schoolboy cricketer, but through strength of will, more than anything else, he became a fine Test batsman and an outstanding captain of Sussex and, fot two matches, of England. The first ordained priest to play Test cricket, he also became Bishop of Liverpool, a member of the House of Lords and was, arguably, the finest Archbishop of Canterbury we never had. When he dropped a few catches on his final tour of Australia in 1962–63 Fred Trueman muttered: 'It's a pity Reverend don't put his hands together more often in t'field.' Usually, though, he was an outstanding close fielder.

In the three seasons 1951–53 Sheppard scored 24 centuries and completed more than 2,000 runs each summer. In 1952, as captain of Cambridge, he topped the national batting averages with 2,262 runs and an average of 64.62, including a career-best 239 not out against Worcester. He was appointed Sussex captain in 1953, at the age of only 24, and after a dodgy start the county led the table in June and July. He led by example and was an inspiring figure on and off the field. Players of that era generally agreed that he was the best captain they played under.

Five players passed 1,000 runs, Sheppard, the junior versions of Jim Parks and George Cox, Ken Suttle and John Langridge, who was now 43. Ian Thomson, in his first full season as a professional, and Ted James each took 100 wickets. There was also reliable twirl from Robin Marlar and, until he broke

Ian Thomson. One of Sussex's all-time greats.

his thumb, Alan Oakman. Surrey were the team to beat in the 1950s, just as Yorkshire had been in the 1930s. From 1952 they won seven successive Championships. In 1953, though, they had the fright of their lives.

Sussex beat them by seven wickets at Guildford, where Sheppard scored a century and James took nine wickets. When they met again, at the end of August, a Sussex win might have brought them the title. Surrey lost three quick wickets, but a dogged innings by David Fletcher led them to a total of 220. Sheppard then declared as soon as Sussex had pulled level. But Surrey, knowing a draw suited their purposes, decided to play out time, and Sussex were unable to dismiss them. Every Sussex player, with the exception of wicketkeeper Rupert Webb, had a bowl as Peter May scored a century. Sussex beat Lancashire by an innings in their final match to make sure of runners-up spot, but members had hoped for so much more. Sheppard made way for Hubert Doggart in 1954 and, in a wet summer, Sussex slid back to ninth position.

Twenty-eight seasons passed before Sussex were second once more and again it took an inspirational captain to take them there. John Barclay, unlike Sheppard, was never an England player, though he was a brave opening batsman, a reliable slip fielder and a thoughtful off-spinner with a pleasing loop. But he did share some of the great man's skills when it came to bringing the best out of his players, who were arguably the best in the Championship that year. Interestingly, there was a link between the two leaders.

In his foreword to *The Longest Journey*, which celebrated Sussex's eventual triumph in 2003, Barclay said: 'I started my relationship with Sussex with David Sheppard on a glorious August day in 1961, when I travelled with my family from Horsham to watch Sussex play cricket at Hove for the first time.

'It was then the traditional bank-holiday match against Middlesex, and we sat on the splintery wooden benches in the south-west corner of the ground.

John Barclay was one of the best post-war captains in Sussex's history.

'Hove was full, or so it seemed, and this impressionable little seven-year-old watched Sheppard make a hundred amidst sunshine and picnic and much happiness. I was captivated by the magical strokeplay, by the majesty and elegance of both class and style. I was hooked and from then on all I wanted was to play cricket and to try to imitate those golden moments of childhood.'

Barclay was faithful to his boyhood promises, and he wrote a most entertaining volume, *The Appeal of the Championship*, about his own efforts to win the title 20 years after watching that innings by Sheppard.

The 1981 vintage was certainly one of the best-balanced sides Sussex had ever put out, with a world-class opening attack, quality seam support, two spinners and a number of attacking batsmen. The most successful of the batsmen were Paul Parker, who would play his only Test match against Australia at The Oval that year, and Gehan Mendis, who probably should have played for England when Graham Gooch was banned in 1982. Gooch certainly thought so. Apart from these two, the batting was inconsistent. But there was depth to make up for it, with a plethora of all-rounders.

Sussex, though, were at their best in the field. The attack was led by Imran Khan and Garth le Roux, backed up by Geoff Arnold, one of the most skilful medium-pacers in the land, and Ian Greig, the find

Gehan Mendis did not play for England but perhaps should have done.

of the season, who probably should have played for England that summer; he had to wait until 1982, when he was less effective. Tony Pigott and the distinctly nippy Adrian Jones were also at the club, and the two spinners, Chris Waller and Barclay himself, played regularly. Barclay took over as captain from Arnold Long that year and drew up his battle plans in the sand of Sydney's Coogee Bay the previous winter while captaining Waverley Cricket Club. Before the start of the season, he and the chief coach, Stewart Storey, took the players off to a hotel in Arundel to get to know each other.

The Championship was between Sussex and Nottinghamshire, and the defining moment of the season came when the two sides met for the only time that summer at Trent Bridge in the middle of August. The pitches there were prepared for Richard Hadlee and Clive Rice, who were every bit as dangerous as Imran and le Roux. There was no shortage of grass. Sussex, though, felt that their seam attack had greater depth and travelled to the Midlands with some confidence. The skilful groundsman changed tack and produced a surface for spinners. They took 20 of the 39 wickets that fell, and Eddie Hemmings, Nottinghamshire's England off-spinner, who finished his career at Hove, took nine of them for 151 runs.

Sussex got the better of the thrilling draw. Put in, they were bowled out for 208 but took the initiative when they dismissed Notts for 102. Second time around, Sussex made 144, with Ian Greig (43) and Ian Gould (42), the wicketkeeper who had joined from Middlesex, their top scorers. Notts were left to score 251 to win on the last day and, when they were 174–3, were clear favourites to get there. That was why they turned down a number of opportunities to leave the field because of bad light. However, they did retreat to the pavilion when they collapsed to 205–7.

When they came back, le Roux dismissed Bruce French and Kevin Cooper with successive deliveries at 210, and Sussex needed just one more wicket. They were convinced that they had won when Imran then beat Mike Bore, hitting him on the shin of his back leg. All the players went up for the lbw shout, but the umpire Peter Stevens, known as 'Shaking' to the Sussex players, gave Bore not out.

Sussex won their last four matches, taking 92 points. But so did Nottinghamshire, winning exactly the same number of points to maintain their slender two-point lead.

In his book, Barclay reflected: 'Our immediate reaction was not one of disappointment, rather of elation. We had aspired to excellence and had played a lot of wonderful cricket along the way. It is only with the passing of time that the disappointment of not winning has grown. I can never quite put it to the back of my mind. The "what ifs" loom larger.'

And so another generation passed. Sussex hardly covered themselves in glory in the years leading up to their first Championship: 14th in 1986, followed by 17th, 16th, 10th, 17th, 11th, seventh, 10th, eighth, 15th, 12th, 18th (for Durham had become the 18th county in 1992), seventh, 11th and, in 2000, ninth. But 2000 was the first year of the split Championship, so their ninth in the Second Division really meant last place once again. They won the Second Division title the following season, were almost relegated when they came sixth in 2002, and then, in 2003, the Holy Grail was seized. That first Championship was also their most emphatic (they won four more matches than anyone else and finished a dizzy 34 points above their closest rivals, Lancashire) but also their most satisfying. In 2006 they were playing away, in Nottingham, and in 2007 they were not on the field but desperately monitoring Lancashire's demise against Surrey at The Oval. On that most memorable of days, on that blessed, sunny afternoon, at 1.43pm on Thursday 18 September 2003, Sussex were on the field and on their way to a famous victory over Leicestershire when the vital, history-making point was grasped. Its inevitability did not make it any less dramatic. Murray Goodwin pulled a short ball from Phil DeFreitas to the midwicket boundary.

Sussex had reached 300 and taken the third batting point they needed to confirm the title. Play was suspended for seven minutes in that fourth over after lunch, and it was as if the world had stopped spinning to take a good look at a green patch of land in Hove. There, the spinning had just started. A bottle of champagne was delivered to the middle of the ground on a silver salver. Kipling's *Sussex by the Sea*, the old First World War quick-march song, seemed to have greater resonance than ever before as it boomed from the tannoy. The umpires, Mervyn Kitchen and Trevor Jesty, looked on, a little bewildered, as the players did a lap of honour. From the committee-room balcony the president Jim Parks, who had been a young member of the 1953 side, glowed with sheer pride. Since the last of their collection of rattling wooden spoons had been won just three years earlier, and they had only just clung on, white-knuckled, to their First Division status in 2002, this moment had not been predicted at the start of the season.

In fact they were generally considered to be 33–1 outsiders, and one bookmaker had them as far out as 50–1. Surrey, the champions of the previous summer, were most people's pick for the title, while Warwickshire, Kent, Lancashire and Leicestershire had also finished ahead of Sussex in 2002. Sussex were sixth that year, and the fact that it was their best placing for six seasons dispelled any notion of disappointment. In fact, it was considered a real achievement after the year had started tragically when the gifted all-rounder Umer Rashid drowned during the club's pre-season tour to Grenada. Three key players, the leading fast bowlers James Kirtley and Jason Lewry, and the captain, Chris Adams, were injured and played just 10 matches apiece. There was trouble off the field, too, with the resignation of chairman Don Trangmar three years ahead of schedule. Just three matches were won.

In 2003, though, there was one crucial difference to the Sussex side: Mushtaq Ahmed had arrived. The Pakistan leg-spinner took 103 wickets, more than any other bowler in the country, and took 10 or more wickets in a match on five occasions. Imran Khan, Mushtaq's old Test captain, had left Hove 15 years before, and when he did so he said that his overseas replacement should be an accomplished wrist-spinner. How right he was. Mushtaq was the first bowler to take 100 first-class wickets in an English season for five years and the first to do so for Sussex since Tony Buss in 1967.

Sussex won the title, moreover, with the smallest squad of players in the country, just 18, and they used just 15 of them. But the most famous season in their history started badly. They were not involved in the first round of Championship matches, though Mushtaq gave a clue as to what was to come with figures of 11–49 against the students of Cardiff UCCE. Then, in their Championship opener at Lord's, Middlesex beat them by three wickets. They regrouped to beat Kent at Hove by 133 runs, but in their next match, at Edgbaston, they played badly and lost to Warwickshire by 234 runs. Even coach Peter Moores, who rarely criticised his players in public, let rip. In their next game, against Nottinghamshire at Horsham, Sussex turned their form around, winning by 10 wickets to move from third from bottom to third from the top in the table. Mushtaq, with six wickets in each innings, was seen as the side's great match-winner at this level for the first time.

Sussex lost their next game, however, and slid to fifth. Surrey beat them by 113 runs at The Oval, though a fine rearguard innings from Michael Yardy almost saved his side. They returned to third in the table at the beginning of June, when they completed the double over Kent, beating them by 191 runs at Tunbridge Wells. But Surrey, followed by Lancashire, still led the Championship. Victory in their next game, against Warwickshire, was celebrated with some enthusiasm because it had been 11 years since they beat the Bears. They took the wicketkeeping gloves off Matt Prior and gave them to Tim Ambrose, and Prior responded by scoring a century. Sussex scored 545 and bowled Warwickshire out for 201 and 285 to win by an innings and 59 runs, with Mushtaq taking seven wickets in the second innings to take his tally to 52 from just seven games. With four wins, Sussex were now second to Surrey. They reached the halfway point in their next match, against Essex on a typically slow Arundel pitch, which they won by six wickets with just 4.1 overs to spare. When they won their next match at Leicester, by five wickets, they cut Surrey's lead to just five points.

Significantly, it was here that Adams rediscovered his form with the bat. He made just 0 and 16, but it was a long net session at Grace Road with Moores which, he said, turned his season round. At Leicester they won in the final session for the third time. They had to settle for a damp draw at Trent Bridge at the end of July and returned to Hove for the crucial match against Surrey, where both Prior and Ambrose were awarded their county caps.

There were gate receipts of over £20,000, a record for a Championship match at Hove. But the large crowd were not happy after Adams delayed his declaration, setting Surrey a target of 377 in 34 overs. Surrey's Saqlain Mushtaq and Ian Salisbury, Sussex players of the future and the past, made their feelings known when they bowled seam-up instead of spin. The match was drawn, and Sussex were criticised for coming off for bad light on the third day when there were 37 overs to bowl. Adams, though, sensed a moral victory.

'Normally, when Surrey play us, they are relaxed because they know that at some stage over the four days they will take control of the game,' he said. 'On the last day here they got in our faces a bit and tried to unsettle us, but I took that as a moral victory for us. It showed that we were breathing down their necks and were prepared to compete with them.'

Surrey certainly felt the heat by the middle of August when Sussex won their seventh match, a thrilling victory over Lancashire at Hove with just 12 minutes to spare with the home side's coaching staff

Murray Goodwin celebrates his magnificent triple hundred in the title-clinching match against Leicestershire in 2003.

patrolling the boundary so that balls that pierced the ring of close fielders were returned more quickly. Adams became only the fourth batsman, after Fry, Ranjitsinhji and John Langridge, to score twin hundreds for the county more than once. Then, on 22 August, Sussex moved to the top of the table for the first time when they beat Essex at Colchester by an innings and 120 runs with more than a day to spare. Murray Goodwin made a then career-best 210, including 101 between lunch and tea, as Sussex scored 612. Essex supporters gave the Sussex players a standing ovation at the end of the match.

By now it was September and with three matches to go the pressure was on Sussex for a change. They responded by beating Middlesex at Hove by seven wickets to go 18 points clear. They were struggling at 107 for six in reply to 392, but then Prior (148) and Mark Davis (168) put on 195, the most important stand of the season. Sussex went to Old Trafford for their penultimate match hoping to clinch the Championship, with Mushtaq also hoping to take his 100th wicket; both aims were unfulfilled. Adams and his men were beaten by an innings and 19 runs and skulked home still needing six points to win the title. With a day lost to rain, Sussex should have managed the draw that would have suited them, but they were betrayed by their nerves and took just four of the 10 points they needed.

'We concentrated too much on getting points rather than playing our normal game,' said Adams. But it was stage fright and timidity that allowed Lancashire to avenge that defeat at Hove and give themselves a chance of winning the Championship outright for the first time since 1934. After this they had taken 63 points from 66.

Sussex only had to avoid the follow-on, but in reply to Lancashire's 450 they collapsed from 122–1 to 157–7. At least they won a second batting point to put Surrey out of the race. And so to the final match against Leicestershire at Hove. Sussex had wanted to bat first on a flat pitch, but when Leicestershire won the toss they were bowled out for 179 in just 69.5 overs. Three bowling points – and just three more required!

Lancashire were playing Nottinghamshire at Trent Bridge and were on a roll, but Sussex knew that whatever happened at Nottingham they needed just three batting points – to reach 300 in their first innings – to secure the great prize. At the close of play on the first day, playing with measured responsibility, they had reached 137 for one and needed 163 more. Surely only rain could deny them now – or perhaps Hurricane Isabel, who was on a world tour. Then Goodwin, on his way to a Sussex record 335 not out, pulled his famous four. Even the older members in the deck-chaired north of the ground cheered and jigged, blankets and Thermoses falling about them, to celebrate a moment their patient forefathers had never seen.

On the third morning, the Friday, Adams was missing with tennis elbow. Vice-captain Kirtley, who had made a successful Test debut in the summer but was missing from this match because of shin-splints, led the side out before heading back to the dressing room. It was

Behind the shades. James Kirtley.

The unmistakable sight of Jason Lewry pounding in.

a touching gesture. The match was not put to bed for some time. Mushtaq was absent, too, and it was not until after tea that victory was completed by 55 runs, following a burst from Jason Lewry, who took five wickets for six runs.

Perhaps the partying in the Sussex Cricketer pub the evening before had taken something out of a few of the players – or put something in! Some members complained that the match should have been wrapped up earlier. When it was, there came another rendition of *Sussex by the Sea*, and Queen's *We Are The Champions* got an airing too. Fireworks exploded as Adams was awarded the Frizzell County Championship trophy. John Carr, Director of Cricket Operations for the England and Wales Cricket Board, fluffed his lines and said: 'Congratulations to Surrey for winning the County Championship.' But he was forgiven. Murder would have been forgiven by most Sussex supporters after the most deliriously enjoyable match in the county's long and patient history.

Chapter 6
One-Day Wonders

BEFORE a big match at Lord's, the great ground can appear as some ocean liner on the brink of its maiden voyage. Boats are often invested with human qualities and Lord's, it seems, preens with pride, clean-decked, flags fluttering and whistles blowing as passengers scurry into place; there is even a bell that clangs outside the members' bar, not to indicate the sailors' duty watches but to herald the start of each session of play. The place, it seems, is self-consciously aware of its considerable importance. By the early summers of the new millennium, however, it was evident that the traditional end-of-season celebration, the game's answer to football's FA Cup Final, had become a little tired.

While the Finals of the Gillette Cup (1963–80) and the NatWest Trophy (1981–2000) are remembered for so many twilight thrillers, it has been Cheltenham & Gloucester's misfortune to preside over something rather less compelling. August is preferred to September now, and it is no longer remotely near the end of the season. There has also been a samey look about proceedings. When Gloucestershire played Worcestershire in 2004 it was a repeat of the previous year's Final. Gloucestershire, in fact, reached four Finals in 1999–2004. In 2003, Gloucestershire beat Worcestershire by seven wickets. In 2004, when there were 7,000 empty seats, the margin was eight wickets.

The 2006 Final, in which Sussex beat Lancashire quite thrillingly in a match between the best two sides in the country, was a throwback to the old summer climaxes. It was fitting that Sussex, the first champions of the competition, should meet the side who stole their one-day mantle in the 1970s. It was also, like some of the earlier Finals, a relatively low-scoring match. And a crowd of almost 24,000 watched, transfixed, as the balance of the contest tilted one way and then the next. It was, according to the Sussex captain Chris Adams, 'The most amazing game I have ever played in. And I know how important it was to the people of Sussex, who still have their scars from 1993 when we last got here.'

James Kirtley celebrates one of his five wickets in the C&G Trophy Final against Lancashire in August 2006.

James Kirtley sinks to his knees after taking Lancashire's last wicket in the 2006 C&G Trophy Final.

James Kirtley disappears under a scrum of Sussex bodies.

Luke Wright grabs a souvenir, while the rest of the Sussex players mob James Kirtley. Lord's, August 2006.

It also had an appropriate hero in James Kirtley. That year the Sussex fast bowler, his match-winning Test debut against South Africa at Trent Bridge in 2003 a distant memory, had remodelled his controversial action, having already overhauled it. He was something of an afterthought in the Championship team that year, playing just seven matches and taking 16 wickets at 40.18 apiece. He only played at Lord's after a bright burst in a Pro40 match against Glamorgan. Jason Lewry may have considered himself unlucky to miss out.

But Kirtley won the Man of the Match award with a devastating return of 5–27, a career best in one-day cricket. All his wickets were lbw, but Stuart Law, a first-ball victim, was unlucky – he got a thick inside edge onto his pads and looked up with horrified incredulity as the umpire raised his finger.

'The great thing about James is that he never stopped working,' said Adams. 'For two hours, five days a week for six months, he worked on his action for this moment. He was in the indoor school at 8.30 every morning in the winter, working at his action.

'He's been through the mill, but I think he's got more character, fight and belief than any cricketer I've ever played with. It was a great day for Sussex but it was really James's day – he was awesome.

'This was the same as winning a Test match for England, an Andrew Flintoff-style performance. People like him don't come along very often.'

This was also a match which underlined the enduring appeal of the 50-over game, which has been threatened to the brink of extinction by its brash younger brother, Twenty20 cricket.

The Sussex batsmen looked nervous – betrayed by their clumpy running between the wickets – when they were put in under heavy clouds. Sajid Mahmood appeared as the England bowler that he has only fitfully shown in international colours, bowling with pace, bounce and movement. His dismal performances against Sri Lanka earlier in the summer looked like an aberration as he took 3–16 in 8.1 overs. In these conditions, Lancashire also had plenty of experienced support in Dominic Cork, Glen Chapple and Kyle Hogg.

'It was a fantastic toss to win,' said Adams. 'I would definitely have bowled. Conditions were awful. The pitch was damp and had plenty of grass on it.'

Sussex crashed to 78–6. Their supporters, for whom glory here had last come 20 years before, looked glum and used their banners for warmth rather than waving in the dispiriting conditions. Two run-outs further undermined their cause. The first was Richard Montgomerie, who departed with just four on the board. Then Matt Prior was caught at mid-on after scoring a rather too impatient 23. In these circumstances Sussex looked to their two best and most experienced batsmen, Adams and Murray Goodwin, and they both failed. Adams, in fact, looked as jittery as anyone and twice might have been run out before he fell for six; Goodwin made one more. There was a distinct lack of composure in the Sussex side.

After Carl Hopkinson had become the second run-out victim and Robin Martin-Jenkins, who was not really out, fell for 15, Michael Yardy was joined by Yasir Arafat. They each made 37 runs, ugly-duckling Yardy from 97 balls and the clean-hitting Arafat from 43. They almost doubled the score, putting on 66. And if Yardy, with his shuffling style, was hardly a thing of beauty on this occasion, he was mightily effective. He hit just one four, but Lancashire's impetus had been broken. The tail did not contribute many runs, but at least Sussex's total of 172 was competitive in the conditions.

Those conditions, however, changed. The skies were less sullen when Lancashire batted and when Mal Loye hoisted Kirtley into the Grand Stand in only the fifth over, red roses bloomed all over Lord's. Two balls later, though, Kirtley hit Loye on the pads, and the batsman – most unusually for an lbw decision and in a match of such importance – walked. Kirtley struck twice in his next over to dismiss Nathan Astle, who was obviously leg-before, and Law, who was unlucky; Lancashire were reeling at 27–3.

Even in these seamer-friendly conditions there was still room for Mushtaq Ahmed's genius. Mixing it up cleverly and never allowing the batsmen to settle, he bowled his 10 overs for 19 runs and claimed the wickets of the Lancashire captain

Mike Yardy is first to congratulate James Kirtley after Sussex ended two decades of waiting for victory in a Lord's Final.

Mushy strikes again. A wicket for the magical leg-spinner at Lord's in the 2006 C&G Trophy Final.

Mark Chilton, who was stumped, and the dangerous Chapple, who was caught at silly mid-off. Cork came to the wicket at 72–6, similar to Sussex's worst position, and together with Hogg he set about playing the same rescuing role that Yardy and Arafat had staged earlier in the day.

They took the score to 130–6 after Hogg had been dropped by Montgomerie: a crucial miss it seemed at the time. With 30 balls and three wickets left the target was only 28. Cork, though, nudged a single from almost every ball, was not his usual free-scoring self, but he was very effective. It was the dogged batting of this bloody-minded cricketer that almost denied Sussex the Championship in 2007. Here, though, he was betrayed by Mahmood, who was bowled by Arafat, swinging wildly. And by now Kirtley had returned to have Tom Smith lbw and then, with 16 runs still needed, he finished the match with his fifth wicket, that of Murali Kartik.

James Kirtley with the C&G Trophy after his match-winning performance in the 2006 Final against Lancashire.

Chris Adams celebrates in traditional manner after becoming the first Sussex captain for 20 years to lift a one-day trophy

'It had been tough for me but this was a reward for the support I've received from everyone at the club for the previous nine months,' Kirtley recalled. 'I had been talking about my action for the previous four or five years, but here I just wanted to perform.

'I think the demons finally disappeared from my head about May time. It's hard enough bowling against top batsmen as it is, but when you have something distracting you, like your action, it's a lot tougher. You can't fight demons and take wickets at the same time.'

Mushtaq was always going to take something more significant than mere cricket from the game: 'Religion is a big part of my life now. I feel much more relaxed in my family life and my cricket. This was my first Final so it was a special experience for me. I was very happy with the way I bowled because I had been really struggling in the three or four weeks before the match. But there was just no time for a rest.'

Yardy had to get special permission to celebrate with the other Sussex players that Saturday night – the following day he had to travel down to Bristol to join up with England's one-day squad.

'That was quite a week for me, the England call-up and then the big win at Lord's,' he said. 'We had the worst of conditions there, but a little bit of cloud cover drifted over when James took the new ball for us, and he took advantage. Lancashire were always on the back foot after that. They had scoreboard pressure and the pressure of chasing. It got to them in the end.'

While Adams and Mushtaq had used raw talent to play Test cricket for their countries, Yardy represented another type of Sussex cricketer, a solid county man who, by maximising his talents, had also gone on to achieve higher honours. There was only one winner of the Man of the Match award at Lord's, but Yardy, an intelligent, thinking cricketer with a diploma in sports psychology, was the man who gave Kirtley and Mushtaq something to bowl at. Just two years before he had been a struggling second-team player, left-handed, dour and one-paced. He supplemented his meagre income by working in a sports shop at Gatwick Airport in the winter.

'I had a net session with Peter Moores, who was then the Sussex coach, a couple of years before that Lord's Final, and I changed my trigger movements. I became a more aggressive player, with more shots. I'm not a David Gower or anything like that. But I can guts it out in difficult situations. I can accumulate runs but now I can also hit the ball when needed.'

With his feet wide apart outside the leg-stump in a very open stance, he wins few points for artistic impression – though by the time the ball arrives he has hopped neatly into line. Against Lancashire, Yardy reverted to his old stodgy style to make his 37. And he followed that up with five overs of slow left-arm (though not very slow) for just 18 runs.

Sussex had won for the fifth time in nine Lord's Finals, and by beating Lancashire they had given themselves a major psychological boost with the run-in to the Championship to come. And amid the Sussex supporters making their way to St John's Wood station after the match could be seen the cheerful, ruddy-faced figure of Jim Parks, one of the county's earlier heroes on this stage.

Sussex were the original masters of one-day cricket when the format was introduced to the county game in 1963. They won the Gillette Cup that year – or 'the First-Class Counties Knock-Out Competition for the Gillette Cup', to give the competition its full and rather unwieldy title. The shorter game was all about who won the toss and who was luckier on the day. Or so many people said. But Sussex, by way of an encore, won the thing again in 1964. In fact they were not defeated in the competition until 23 June 1965, when Middlesex beat them in a third-round match at Lord's. Their success owed much to the imagination of their captain, Ted Dexter. But Dexter, however well he batted and led the side, was not uncritical about the new toy of limited-over cricket.

In his 1966 book, *Ted Dexter Declares*, he wrote: 'This one-day affair certainly bucked up the Sussex side and presented me, happily, with a new intriguing problem to solve. I confess at once that the limited-over game does not appeal to me much, it makes for stereotyped bowling, and after all the art of bowling is as much a part of the game as the possibly more eye-catching art of batting.'

Matches were played over 65 overs in that first year of 1963 and, despite the sponsorship, the competition was run on a shoestring. The players were often put up in private houses – often the homes of committee members – to save hotel expenses. Nevertheless, the game was entering a fresh epoch. The last Gentleman versus Players match, the ancient contest between the game's amateurs and professionals, had been played in September 1962. That year also saw the introduction of the Cavaliers, a first look at the new biff-bang game for many people. Some reflect that 1962–63 represented the real start of the 1960s. These matters are not decided by diaries and calendars, and you will get a different answer from a sportsman, a politician, a fashion designer and a car manufacturer. Even politics sounded exciting in the early 1960s, with Harold Wilson, the new Labour leader, banging on about the 'white heat of technology'. To amend the words of the other political Harold – Macmillan – Sussex had never had it so good when one-day cricket got under way. But the same could not be said about the game in general at that time.

Ted Dexter finds the boundary in one of his last games against the touring Australians at Arundel in 1972.

The Gillette Cup came into being in 1963 because the game's finances were in a bad way. The public interest in both county and Test cricket had declined throughout the 1950s – Championship gates were almost two million in 1950 but had declined to 700,000 in 1963. A knock-out competition had been discussed as early as 1957, when an MCC committee met to discuss declining gates and the tempo of the game. The 1960s would also see the introduction of the John Player (Sunday) League in 1969, which was followed, three years later, by the Benson and Hedges Cup and, another three years later, by the first World Cup. Overseas players, including all-time great cricketers like Garry Sobers, Clive Lloyd, Barry Richards, Mike Procter and Greg Chappell, flooded into the county game in 1968, so domestic game cricket, like much else in life, underwent radical change in that decade. When the Gillette Cup started 45 years ago, many said the experiment would not work because it was too inclined to be frivolous. What would those people have said about the Twenty20 game?

Sussex, though, by accident and design, were well suited to the demands of the new format. They may have lacked a quality spinner, but that was not a terrible handicap in this form of cricket. It was the dashing batting of Dexter and Parks that usually caught the headlines in 1963 and 1964, but it was the fast and fast-medium bowlers, operating with defensive fields, who were the key players in those days, when scores were considerably lower than they are in modern slogathons, with advanced bat technology, shortened boundaries and a generally more aggressive approach to the game. The young John Snow and the experienced Ian Thomson, Tony Buss and Don Bates were the key performers in this area, backed up by Dexter's occasional medium-pace and the part-time twirl of Alan Oakman and Ken Suttle. So, by accident, they had the right players for the new task. The design came from Dexter. Here was one of the most attacking cricketers of his or any other time. But, before anyone else, he realised that the new form of cricket was, essentially, a defensive game. His insightful tactics did not always go down well, while others were still trying to work out how to play it.

In his book, Dexter wrote: 'Sussex won two Gillette Cups before the other counties had woken up to the problem. I remember the first game against Kent at Tunbridge Wells. We won the toss and Colin Cowdrey set a very friendly field indeed.

'We made a big score (314–7); it was all very sporting and pleased the big crowd. Kent went in and the picture changed dramatically. There was only one man who looked like doing any good and that was Peter Richardson.

'It was not my main intention to get him out. I just set the field back, allowed him to take a single, then bowled tight to the other batsman to force him to make the runs and not Richardson.

'There were boos and screams, and everyone thought that this was a rotten thing to do – there was so much sympathy for Richardson that he received the team [Man of the Match] award – but there it was, I had shown people what they could be let in for.'

Parks agrees that Dexter worked out the game while everyone else was still pondering over how to play it: 'After that game at Tunbridge Wells the chairman of Kent wrote to the chairman of Sussex saying how disgusted he was. But, tactically, Ted was spot on.

'I remember Colin Cowdrey persevering with two slips and a gully right the way through our innings. When we went in the field we had just the one slip from the start.'

Sussex went on to reach the Final again in 1968 (beaten by Warwickshire), 1970 (beaten by Lancashire, who were to become the new champions of the limited-over game in that decade) and 1973, when they were defeated by Procter's Gloucestershire. But Sussex returned to win the premier one-day competition in 1978 and again in 1986 and 2006. And, of course, they also lost an astonishing final against Warwickshire in 1993 after scoring 321–6, a record for a Cup Final. That day belonged to Asif Din and Dermot Reeve, but Sussex knew they should have won. At the time, this match was considered by many people the greatest one-day game that had ever been played.

Given their success in the most glamorous of the domestic one-day competitions – at least until the success and popularity of Twenty20 cricket – it is surprising that Sussex fared less well in other forms of the game. They did not even reach the Final of the old Benson and Hedges Cup, which started in 1972, and only made the semi-final on two occasions, in 1982 and 1999. Their performances in the early summers of the Twenty20 Cup were also disappointing. But there was another one-day triumph. In 1982, by way of making up for their bitter disappointment in the Championship the previous year, they won the Sunday League.

1963

This was the year Henry Cooper dumped Cassius Clay (who was yet to become Muhammad Ali) on the seat of his pants with the sweetest of left hooks. Someone called Alf Ramsey became England's football manager, while in cricket Colin Cowdrey went to the crease at Lord's, batting with a broken arm to oversee one of the game's most memorable draws.

After their victory over Kent in the opening round of the Gillette Cup, Sussex played Yorkshire in front of 15,000 at Hove. Parks won the Man of the Match award for his 90, and he was well supported by Richard Langridge (56) and Dexter (44) in a total of 292. They won by 22 runs when Yorkshire were dismissed for 270 (Geoff Boycott top-scoring with 71). Sussex made 292 again in their semi-final against Northants at Hove (Dexter 115, Parks 71, Les Lenham 41) before Thomson (4–33) and Dexter (3–40) bowled out the hosts for 187 to win by 105 runs. Then, in the Final, they beat Worcestershire by just 14 runs. Batting first, as they had done in each round, they scored just 168 on the damp pitch.

The shape of a one-day side was different in those days. The batting was opened by the gangling figure of Alan Oakman, a fluent driver but hardly a pinch-hitter, and Richard Langridge, a naturally slow scorer. In difficult conditions, however, Langridge, a plodding front-foot player who seemed to possess the peculiar ability to run on his heels, scored a crucial 34 in an opening stand of 62. They then slumped to 98–4, with Dexter making three, and only reached the total they did because of a fighting half-century from Parks, who was a particularly fine player of spin bowling. Seven Sussex players failed to reach double figures, and the total did not look big enough against a side good enough to win the County Championship in 1964 and 1965. When Worcestershire were 80–2, with Tom Graveney at the wicket, they looked well placed. But they lost four wickets for five runs as Snow finished off the tail.

Parks should have won the Man of the Match award. But the legendary pair of Frank Woolley and Herbert Sutcliffe decided to give the prize to Worcestershire's captain Norman Gifford (4–33). Sussex, though, did pick up the winners' cheque from Gillette worth £1,889. After 125 years they had actually won something.

Jim Parks remembered: 'It had rained all week, and Lord's was sodden. We thought there might not be any play. The conditions gave Worcestershire a great advantage because they had two specialist slow left-armers in Norman Gifford and Doug Slade and we didn't have a specialist spinner. We didn't play Ronnie Bell, our left-arm spinner.

'Ted had a typical piece of inspiration when he decided to bowl Alan Oakman's little off-breaks. Oaky bowled 13 overs for 17 runs and took the crucial wicket of Tom Graveney.

'We didn't know whether we had scored enough, but we bowled and fielded well enough in the end and the game ended in near darkness.

'My abiding memory of that match is the photograph which shows last man Jack Flavell losing his middle stump to John Snow. You can't see the batsman in the picture – just this shot of the wicket with the middle one flying out of the ground!'

1964

Harold Wilson won a general election for the first time, Mary Rand and Ann Packer won gold in the Tokyo Olympics and Fred Trueman became the first bowler to take 300 Test wickets. Experts asked themselves whether his record would ever be broken.

In the Gillette Cup, the prize money had gone up to £2,167 17s 6d when Sussex retained the trophy by beating Warwickshire. The club was more interested in the gate money. In 1964 fewer than 36,000 people watched Sussex, compared with 42,000 in the comparatively damp and miserable summer of 1963. Sussex beat a minor county called Durham by 200 runs at Hove in the second round but nearly came unstuck on a fast pitch at Taunton in the third when Somerset's Geoff Hall (5–34) and Fred Rumsey (4–19) bowled them out for 141. Dexter and Parks were both gone in the first 10 overs. But Somerset, despite Roy Virgin's 54, could muster only 125.

In the semi-final Sussex beat Surrey by 90 runs. Dexter, who did not make a big score in his three Lord's Finals, was Man of the Match for his 84 and 3–17. Hundreds were locked out of the Hove ground. Despite indifferent form in the Championship (Sussex were ninth that year) the supporters had clearly taken to the one-day game. In the Final they played Warwickshire. Warwickshire already knew something about Thomson, who after Maurice Tate was probably the best medium-pace bowler to represent the county. He was 43 when he last played for the county in 1972, but was probably at his peak in 1964 when his in-dippers and leg-cutters took 115 wickets at 16.02. There were some who compared him to Alec Bedser, but Thomson should be regarded as a very fine bowler in his own right. At Worthing in June he took all 10 Warwickshire wickets in the first innings and followed that with five in the second for match figures of 15–75. Sussex lost the match after being bowled out for 23 in their second innings.

In the Lord's Final, Warwickshire captain Mike Smith won the toss and batted, only to see Thomson remove his top three batsmen with only 21 on the board. Warwickshire never really recovered and were bowled out for 127. *The Cricketer* Magazine praised Thomson for his 'accuracy, prodigious movement and cleverly disguised changes of pace', and noted that it was unlikely that Warwickshire's seamers would have bowled as well. Thomson finished with 4–23 and was well supported by Snow (2–28) and Dexter (3–6 in five overs). Sussex romped home by eight wickets. Openers Ken Suttle and Les Lenham each scored forties in an opening stand of 92 and there was little left to do for the not-out batsmen Dexter and Parks.

Thomson, who will be 80 in 2009 but has only recently retired as a supply teacher, said: 'That was the highlight of my career as a Sussex player. Conditions were good for bowling, and the fact that we started early in the morning, 10.45, helped the ball move about a bit. In fact it swung like mad. It was a hazy morning. It must have been a difficult decision for Mike Smith to know whether to bat or bowl.

'The fact that I had so much success against Warwickshire that season must have helped me get on the boat for England's tour of South Africa that winter, where Smith was captain.

'But when we batted, Tom Cartwright, who was a great bowler for them, couldn't make the ball swing at all. He was a good mate of mine, and we often had a chuckle about that.

'We didn't need many, and it was all over by mid-afternoon. I remember when Kenny Suttle got out and said "I bet they were glad to see the back of me – they're all waiting to see Ted Dexter bat." But by the time Ted came to the wicket we didn't need many.

'The county's recent successes have really delighted me. If we'd had a world-class spinner like Mushtaq in my time we would have won the Championship before – certainly in 1953. When the wickets were dry and dusty, and looking good for the spinners, they often put me on because there was no one else.'

1978

Bjorn Borg won the third of his five Wimbledon titles, Martina Navratilova was the winner among the ladies, Mario Kempes drove Argentina to victory in the football World Cup and David Gower made his Test debut. These were glorious days for Sussex sport, with boxer Alan Minter and runner Steve Ovett in the headlines. Things were even looking up for Brighton & Hove Albion.

However, it threatened to be one of the unhappiest seasons in the history of Sussex CCC. The year before had been difficult enough. With names such as Javed Miandad, Imran Khan, Kepler Wessels, John Snow and Tony Greig around the place, in addition to such fine county pros as Paul Parker, John Barclay and Gehan Mendis, 1977 had promised riches. But then Kerry Packer came along and, somehow, Sussex seemed to take that schism personally. Greig was Packer's leading man in England, and Snow and Imran also signed up. There was a pervading mood of gloom around Hove that matched the awful weather. By 1978 Snow had gone. So had Wessels, and Greig left in mid-season, as did Mike Buss. Arnold Long was the captain now. It was a new era and, with injuries and a distinct air of pessimism about the place, it did not promise to be a rich one.

In 1978 Sussex won only four of their 24 first-class matches, losing eight. At one stage it looked likely that they would finish bottom of the Championship. But they found some form in the second half of the season and finished ninth. Their one-day cricket got better too. In the Gillette Cup they eased past Suffolk in the first round but Staffordshire, who were beaten by two runs after needing just 12 from the last three overs, gave them a fright in the second. In the quarter-finals they played Yorkshire at Headingley. Yorkshire made 174–7 on the first day, but heavy rain forced an abandonment and Sussex won a 10-over match thanks to improvised batting from Miandad and some fine fast bowling from Imran and Geoff Arnold.

In the semi-final at Hove a third wicket stand of 123 in 29 overs between Miandad and Parker was the foundation of their 136-run victory over Lancashire. In the Final, Somerset, with Viv Richards, Ian Botham and Joel Garner, were the hot tip to win the first trophy in the county's history. Sussex, though, won their third Lord's Final with something to spare. The obvious strength of Somerset's batting did not deter Long from choosing to field, though when Brian Rose crunched three boundaries from Imran's opening over, which cost 14 runs, he may have had doubts about his decision.

Imran removed Peter Denning's off-stump for a duck, and then Richards came in to play an unusually restrained innings before he was caught on the deep square-leg boundary. Botham played more to type and twice hooked the spinner, Giles Cheatle, for six. Botham was close to his best in an innings of 80, but Barclay, who bowled 12 overs of off-spin and took 2–21, was outstanding.

Sussex required 208 and looked in control of the match once Barclay and Mendis had put on 93 for the first wicket. But then Botham and Joel Garner got among the wickets, and Sussex were tottering at 110–4 before an accomplished and unbeaten 62 from Parker saw them over the line. Mendis, now aged 53 and living south of Manchester, recalled: 'My relationship with Arnold Long, the Sussex captain, was not the most harmonious, to put it mildly. But I must say that he backed me on this occasion.

'I hadn't played – not even picked up a bat – for ages because of a thumb injury. We had this aged, old physio called Bert Parker, and he bowled to me underarm, very gently. I remember asking him "Do you think Big Bird Garner will be bowling to me like this?"

'It was a gamble, and I was dropped, hooking, first ball. But after that Trout [John Barclay] and myself settled down and played really well.'

Mendis was born in Sri Lanka but was England-qualified. When Graham Gooch was banned for three years following his rebel tour of South Africa in 1982, he nominated Mendis as the man who should replace him in the Test side. But it did not happen.

Mendis concluded: 'We're just a lot of old cronies compared with what Chris Adams and these lads have achieved. It's what you have on the mantelpiece at the end of the day which counts, and today's players have plenty of that.'

1982

Bobby Robson succeeded Ron Greenwood as England football manager following the World Cup Finals in Spain (won by Paolo Rossi's Italy), England's rebel cricketers returned from South Africa and Ian Botham scored a wonderful double century against India at The Oval.

For Sussex, it was a season of great optimism, following their heart-breaking failure to win their first Championship the season before. But they finished in eighth place. Imran Khan, who was with Pakistan for most of the summer, could never be replaced, and it was a disappointing, inconsistent season for most of the batsmen. The Sunday League, though, represented a great consolation prize. They not only won it but did so with some élan. They lost only one match, to Worcestershire in June, and finished 12 points ahead of the runners-up, Middlesex. Their tally of 58 points was a record for the John Player League, as was their haul of 14 victories. The prize was won at Hove on 29 August in front of 6,500 supporters, which was a record for the ground in this competition. By winning the match, they went 12 points clear with only two matches to play.

Mendis hit nine fours in a sparkling century and put on 134 for the first wicket with Ian Gould (58) to propel Sussex to a score of 228. It was a good effort against a typically parsimonious John Emburey, whose eight overs cost just 20 runs. Middlesex, though, gave Sussex a fright. Despite good bowling from Garth le Roux, Ian Greig and Tony Pigott, they were in touch with the required run rate until they fell away at the end.

Paul Parker, 52 and now a housemaster at Tonbridge School, where he teaches Latin, recalled: 'It was that Middlesex match which was crucial because they could have caught us. I remember Mendo [Gehan Mendis] and Gunner [Ian Gould] putting us on our way with a really good stand at the top of the order. Roland Butcher was the only one capable of winning it for them, and Butch skied one to me at backward square-leg off John Barclay.

'I thought "you beauty" as I clutched the ball, but then it burst out of my hands, hit me on the head and fell to earth. I had a real stinker in the field that day.' (At this time Parker, especially in the covers, was considered to be just about the most brilliant fielder in England.)

'At the end I ran out John Emburey, who went for a very optimistic run. As he left the field I asked him why he had run, and he said that I was having such a bad time in the field he thought I would miss that one too!'

1986

Diego Maradona's 'Hand of God', which he has only recently owned up to, cheated England out of a possible place in the semi-final of the soccer World Cup, and the England cricket team, under Mike Gatting, set off for Australia on one of the most successful tours in their history.

Sussex were once again looking for some autumn redemption after another disappointing season in the Championship, in which they finished 14th. Imran was still a world-class all-rounder and topped both batting and bowling averages in the Championship. But he played only 10 games. Garth le Roux was not quite the force he had been and only two batsman, Parker and Allan Green, reached 1,000 runs. In the NatWest Bank Trophy, however, they carried all before them. As in 1978, Suffolk provided them with little more than a warm-up match in the opening round and were brushed aside by seven wickets. The second round was more of a challenge, with Green scoring his first century in one-day cricket in Sussex's total of 269–8 at Hove; Glamorgan were bowled out for 240.

In the rain-hit quarter-final at Headingley, which was spread over two days, Ian Gould's score of 88 represented the winning margin, and in the semi-final Worcestershire, like Yorkshire in the previous game,

The Sussex squad in 1986 look tailor-made for success.

Allan Green is stumped for 62 by Lancashire's Chris Maynard in the 1986 NatWest Final.

scored only 125. Imran, once a Worcestershire player, took three wickets for six in five overs and won the Man of the Match award. Sussex and Lancashire, the two most successful counties in the history of the competition, met in the Final. On this occasion the little medium-pacers of Dermot Reeve, such a great performer in Lord's Finals, outshone the pace and bounce of the great Imran. Reeve took four wickets for 12 runs in 25 balls as Lancashire, who had responded to being put in by putting on 50 for the first wicket, saw their middle order blown away. Neil Fairbrother (63) and Andy Hayhurst (49) put on 103 in 20 overs after Clive Lloyd, who received a standing ovation, had been blown away for a duck.

A target of 243 looked sizeable (one-day scores, remember, were more modest 20 years ago), but Sussex crossed the line with something of a swagger. They got there with seven wickets and 10 balls to spare. Allan Green scored 62 and Parker a delightful 85, full of rich strokes that would have graced any form of the game. He suffered cramp but chose to take salt tablets instead of asking for a runner. These two put on 137 for the second wicket, and when they were out Imran Khan dashed Lancashire's revived hopes with an elegant and unbeaten half century.

Tony Pigott, 50 this year and now working in insurance, said: 'Lancashire had been a great side but they were poor in 1986. It was a big surprise when they beat Surrey in the semis, though only by four runs.'

Pigott, who did the hat-trick for his first three wickets in county cricket and went on to play a Test in New Zealand even though he was not a member of the original touring party, added: 'We thought their West Indian fast bowler Patrick Patterson was going to play in the Final, but Clive Lloyd played instead, and he was coming to the end of his career.

Ian Gould holds aloft the NatWest Trophy after Sussex beat Lancashire at Lord's in 1986.

'It was one-sided and might have been more so because we had them five down for a hundred. I remember a lovely innings for us by Allan Green. Mike Brearley said he was the best timer of a cricket ball in England. But then Norman Gifford arrived as coach, and he didn't rate him. That's what can happen in this game.'

In the game of one-day cricket Sussex had won again. And things were going to get even better.

Chapter 7
Robin Marlar – the Maverick

EVEN on a bitterly cold and windswept March afternoon, the home of the man who helped save Sussex County Cricket Club is a hugely impressive pile. It is just outside Guildford in Surrey, although he has another hugely impressive pile in the south of France, where these days he spends most of his winters with his wife, Gill. On this dank, forbidding afternoon one half expected the door to be opened by Boris Karloff or Vincent Price. But it was Robin Marlar. Marlar, 77, has been associated with Sussex County Cricket Club for almost 60 years and has worn more hats than a mad milliner. He was a match-winning spinner – and Sussex have had precious few of those – a captain, committee member, chairman and president. But it was in another, less official role, leading into his chairmanship, that he made his greatest contribution to the recent renaissance of the club.

'Please don't overstate my role in all of this,' said Marlar – a substantial figure in every sense – as he prodded the fire into sparks-flying life. 'But what I can tell you is that what Sussex have achieved in recent years has been a an absolutely fantastic source of joy for an old fart like me. It's unbelievably satisfying. We might be the oldest county in the country but, boy, have we been late developers!'

It is difficult to read anything about Marlar without encountering the word 'maverick.' Infamously, he once went in to bat as night-watchman against Surrey and was stumped, second ball, for six. But it was his vigour and strength of personality, qualities that had made him required reading in the pages of *The Sunday Times,* that would make him a highly effective president of the MCC in 2005–2006, a period of profound change for the county, which helped quieter allies, such as Jim May and Tony Pigott, sweep the old Sussex guard from power in the Empress Ballroom of Brighton's great liner of a seafront hotel, The Grand, on 19 March 1997.

Marlar prefers to haul the rather unsung figure of May into the foreground. May, bespectacled, with a naturally serious countenance that disguises a healthy sense of humour, looks every inch the retired banker and former local councillor he is. And he is the man responsible for getting Marlar involved.

'Jim is a very big boy in everything that happened,' said Marlar. 'He is a man of considerable parts. He is a non-cricketer but the club owes everything to him. He deserves all the credit. Him and the captain.

'We had lost six first-team players in a very short space of time, and I had appeared on TV and said it was absolutely dreadful. If you lose so many players in such a short space of time you should be ashamed of yourselves, and that's what I said.

'When I got back home I took a phone call from Jim. He told me that I had a big mouth and that I should do something with it.

'"Why don't you put up or shut up?" he wanted to know. That was the beginning of everything. That phone call.

'So we met and decided that we should both put up for the committee. Alan Caffyn had resigned as chairman and sent a hospital pass to dear old Ken Hopkins – a nicer chap you'd never meet.

'Jim and I knew we had the popular vote and went to see Hopkins. We said we were not prepared to accept compromises and "You've got to go, all of you," we told them, "or we will oppose you in public."'

Marlar and May had joined forces with Sussex 2000 – 'a pressure group that was making a lot of noise but not doing much.'

'Marlar had been a successful businessman. He had owned his own head-hunting company and knew a thing or two about annual general meetings. The critical element, and this has not come out before, was not to allow any protest to come under any other business at the AGM. We decided to go in at the chairman's report. We proposed an amendment to the chairman's report that the membership shouldn't accept it and from that moment they were done. That was it. Crucially, we had moved the issue from Any Other Business, by which time the head of steam at the meeting would have disappeared, to near the top of the agenda when people still felt bloody angry.'

Marlar became chairman, Tony Pigott was appointed chief executive, Peter Moores became captain...and Sussex finished bottom of the Championship table.

'I had only wanted to be chairman for a year. But I said that I didn't want to go out when we were at the bottom. So I did another year and we moved up to seventh. I never made any secret of the fact that I didn't like committees. I didn't mind being chairman when there were three committee men, but we had to follow the constitution of the club and elect another nine.

'I also upset various members of the committee because I couldn't stand being at Eaton Road in Hove. I wanted to get out of the place. I still do. It's an absolutely hopeless site. I've always believed that if you want to make a success out of a cricket club you have to accommodate the car because the majority of support is going to come from older people. They are going to use their cars, their moveable campsites if you like, and they have to be able to park the bleeder. Kent have always been able to make money because they've always had massive car-parking space.'

Marlar knew that Chris Adams was the man he wanted to captain Sussex: 'It was one incident that persuaded me that Chris was the man. It was during the Benson & Hedges Cup Final between Derbyshire and Lancashire in 1993. Wasim Akram bowled Adams, who was with Derbyshire at the time, a beamer and it was the most deliberate beamer I ever saw in my life.

'Adams's reaction was to come down the wicket holding his bat above his head like a hatchet. And I thought "I like that." Later, I was told that he went up to Wasim in the dining room and told him that if he ever did that again he would kill him. I thought to myself that this chap Adams was the guy we wanted.

Shane Warne has words with Chris Adams, one of many heated confrontations between the captains of Sussex and

'Beamers have played a big part in my life. Nobody has ever written about this, but after the war we just didn't have bowlers who were quick enough to bowl bouncers. We had good cricketers and bright people in men like Trevor Bailey and John Warr, but they couldn't bowl bouncers. Nor could Dick Pollard. And Alec Bedser couldn't bowl a bouncer to save his life.

'If they tried it would turn out to be a long-hop on English pitches. So opening bowlers decided to take the aerial route. There was nothing accidental about it. It was a deliberate policy. At least until John Warr bowled one to Denis Compton in a Gents versus Players match at Lord's. You've never seen anything like it in your life. Denis's bat flew out of his hands, his gloves came off, he stomped around the wicket. I picked up the ball at long leg. It was that one incident that decided the complete unacceptability of the beamer. Until then we had let one go every other game.

'So when I saw Wasim bowl one to Adams I knew exactly what he was doing, and I was delighted by the batsman's reaction.'

But Marlar admits that he was not sure about Peter Moores: 'I did have a bit of a hang-up about Peter. Basically, I thought he was a journeyman. Martin Speight, who left for Durham in 1997, could bat like an angel.

'Peter was a very strong character and a great professional, and those qualities have got him where he is today. He's done a great job. But the raw materials were frankly not good enough for him to be a first-team cricketer, in my opinion.

'We had lunch together at Withdean Stadium, and I will never forget it. Nor will he. We both had our say about life. I told him that he wasn't a very good player and that he'd been bloody lucky, basically. And he, in turn, convinced me that he was absolutely devoted to Sussex cricket, and I bought that. And he was. He bloody well was. He's a terrific team man. So he became captain in that very difficult first year.

'We had Desmond Haynes in charge as coach by then, a lovely chap and a top player but hopeless as a coach. It was an awful appointment, terrible, and it cost us £55,000 to get rid of him. Peter started the next year, 1998, as captain and then said he wanted to do something else, and he was absolutely wonderful as coach.'

The idea of being the club chairman and looking for a captain must have felt a long way away almost half a century earlier. Marlar, who was an amateur cricketer, was educated at Harrow and Cambridge University. He first played for Sussex in 1951, going on to make 223 appearances for the county. In his second season, 1952, he took 108 wickets, 56 of them for Sussex, and for the rest of the decade he would be recognised as one of the foremost off-spinners in the country. He was unlucky to play at a time when England had a number of outstanding off-break bowlers, most notably Jim Laker. Marlar took 15–119 runs against Lancashire at Hove in 1955 and 15–133 against Glamorgan at Swansea in 1952.

His first full season with the club was in 1954, under Hubert Doggart. When Doggart returned to teaching, Marlar was made captain in 1955 and led the county to fourth place. He kept the job until the end of the 1959 season, when he handed over to Ted Dexter.

'The whole point was that in my day we wanted to have fun and play as well as we could, but we weren't killers. I remember having a fantastic argument with Bob Berry, the old Lancashire and England spinner, in a pub in Manchester. We sank pint after pint that night. Bob, with a Lancashire accent you could cut with a knife, was saying how important winning was, and I was saying that I didn't mind if we won or lost, so long as we enjoyed it. It was a totally different attitude.

'David Sheppard was tough, though, a big winner. And we nearly won the title under his captaincy in 1953. I was convinced we were going to win it that year, but we had an unusually bad August and our chance slipped away.'

Marlar had a hand in the appointment of another Sussex captain 40 years ago, when he made a comeback to the colours and played two Championship matches.

'I had really retired from full-time cricket in 1959. I did play a few games in 1960, but by then I had decided to move into other areas.

'But there was a problem at Sussex in 1968. The players had more or less told the cricket committee that they wouldn't play under Jim Parks any more. Jim hadn't done anything wrong. I had played with Jim and marvelled at his talent since I was 16. He was also a first-class bloke. But the players were a revolutionary lot in those days. I was launched in another career by then, but I decided to play in order to have a look for someone who might be capable of taking over. And that someone was Mike Griffith, and he kept the job for a number of years.'

After his pivotal two-year chairmanship of Sussex, Marlar was not lost to the game. He continued to be a regular visitor to Hove and in 2005 was elected the club's president. He was then made president of the MCC in 2005–06. Not long into the job he caused a stir by speaking out against mixed-sex cricket teams.

'It is absolutely outrageous that girls play cricket with boys,' he said. 'Did you know that Brighton College are playing girls in the first XI? Girls! I think it's absolutely outrageous. If there is an 18-year-old who can bowl at 80mph and he's been brought up properly, then he shouldn't want to hurt a lady at any cost.'

Former England women's captain Rachel Heyhoe-Flint, the first woman to be elected onto the MCC committee, said 'Robin is just being a gentleman.' But Clare Connor, the first girl to play for the Brighton College first XI, described his comments as 'Absurd, old-fashioned and patronising.' Connor went on to captain the England women's team to Ashes success in 2005, after which she was awarded the OBE.

Perhaps the greatest thing about Marlar, though, is that he is not frightened to speak and write his singular mind. He doesn't mind upsetting people, and it was that quality that made him such a key mover in 1997. The subsequent winning of three Championships still brings a broad smile to his face. 'It's magic, isn't it? Really. Total magic.'

In 2003 somebody asked Marlar what it felt like to win the title at last: 'I referred them to Lewis Carroll, because he said it all: "Twas brillig." And as for that Thursday and Friday at Hove, when the Jabberwock, the demon who stood between Sussex and victory, had been finally slain, "Oh frabjous day! Callooh! Callay! We chortled our joy." We were champions at long, long last.'

* * * * *

The British are not revolutionary folk. If we were we might have found good reason to torch Downing Street during the Callaghan/Thatcher/Major/Blair years, depending on our political leanings. Our Latin cousins might not have shown the same self-restraint. Even those staunch republicans among us would be deferential, even fawning, if the Queen sauntered into our local looking for a quick half between appointments (with her mother, of course, this would have felt perfectly normal).

We are not exactly timid. On the contrary, we can be a jingoistic, even aggressive race. We are scarcely war-shy, even when its legality is in question and the chances of victory are doubtful. We are quite capable of invading another country at the drop of a sergeant-major's swagger stick. And, in residential terms at least, we are still colonising some of the world's more attractive watering holes. But we are not revolutionary by nature. Perhaps we prefer to internalise our grievances, to sulk and grow angry ulcers and, if really pushed, write cross little letters to *The Times* or send emails to Radio 4's *Today* and *PM* programmes.

In Sussex, where people were growing old long before anyone muttered anything about a changing demographic, this might be particularly true. The membership of Sussex County Cricket Club includes a large number of those who have become accustomed to the deckchair's gentle curve and who do not necessarily march to the Eaton Road ground wearing Che Guevara T-shirts. Yet it was a revolution, of sorts, that propelled Sussex to their recent, unprecedented success. Nor was it a revolution without precedent.

There are some long-toothed members who can recall the events of March 1950, when an angry meeting at the Royal Pavilion reached an acrimonious climax with the resignation of the club's president, the Duke of Norfolk. He stomped out, and so did the committee after a vote of no confidence. Then, the squabble centred around the decision to replace the captain, Hugh Bartlett, with joint captains R.G. Hunt and G.H.G. Doggart. Billy Griffith, the secretary, also resigned in the turmoil. Ultimately, James Langridge was appointed captain, a new committee was elected and the Duke of Norfolk remained as president.

Forty-seven years later it was a slow-burn revolt. Some trace it back to the NatWest Final of 1993. This was, according to a number of sages, the finest one-day game ever played, at least up until that time. The events of 4 September 1993 still ache in the heart of every Sussex supporter. The NatWest, or the Gillette Cup, its original name, or the C&G Trophy, which it became, is a tournament close to the club's heart. While the Holy Grail of the Championship was being pursued, the winning of a clutch of one-day titles, most notably the Gillette Cup in 1963 and 1964, had represented substantial consolation prizes.

Sussex took a talented side to play Warwickshire in 1993. It was hardly the neutrals' favourite contest – they would have preferred to see Somerset and Glamorgan emerge from the semi-finals, to see the wonderful Viv Richards playing against the county that had helped to make his reputation as the most destructive batsman in the world. By the end of this astonishing day, though, the neutrals were delighted. So were the Warwickshire supporters. Sussex had scored a then one-day record of 321 for six from their 60 overs. It was a total Sussex should have defended, without detracting from the efforts of Asif Din and former Sussex player Dermot Reeve in the Warwickshire side. The Sussex bowling and fielding was uninspired, and here was clear evidence that they had the wrong captain in Alan Wells. Wells was a fine batsman, at county level at least. He might even have won more than the solitary England cap that came his way in 1995. But he was not an outstanding leader of men.

Warwickshire won the match off the last ball of the day. Peter Moores, who would replace Wells as captain, was convinced that victory here would have represented a launching pad for an emerging side. Instead, matters got gradually worse. In 1994 they finished eighth in the Championship but lost in the first rounds of the NatWest Trophy and Benson and Hedges Cup, and won only five Sunday League matches. In 1995 they finished 15th in the Championship, and there was no glory on the one-day front. Matters were coming to a rancorous head, and in the middle of the season Norman Gifford resigned after seven years in charge. He was replaced the following winter by Desmond Haynes, the former West Indies opening batsman.

The new year, 1996, was bright with optimism, but matters got even worse. At the end of May, fast bowler Ed Giddins failed a random drugs test during the match against Kent at Tunbridge Wells. The Test and County Cricket Board (now the England and Wales Cricket Board) found him guilty of using a prohibited substance, cocaine, and Sussex sacked him. Meanwhile, there was disunity in the dressing room, where the captaincy of Alan Wells was more unpopular than ever. Sussex, it has to be said, were considered something of a soft touch by the other counties.

David Gilbert, who was to join Sussex but who was then cricket manager at Surrey, said: 'The Sussex side at the time was very experienced, with guys like David Smith, Ian Salisbury and Peter Moores, and emerging players like Jason Lewry. But we always felt they were captained by someone out of touch with his team. We knew that if we put them under any sort of pressure they would buckle, simply because they didn't want to do it for Alan Wells.'

Wells returned from a benefit tour of Barbados in October to be told that Moores, one of his best friends in the game, would replace him as captain in 1997. Alan Caffyn, the club chairman, said 'When we eventually replaced Alan Wells with Peter Moores all the players, almost to a man, said "Thank goodness he's gone!" They admired him as a player but didn't like his captaincy at all.'

Moores said: 'Things had been building up for a while, and you knew at some stage that it would blow up.' He tried to persuade Wells to play on, but he signed a contract with Kent. So Moores had lost two of his most experienced players in Giddins and Wells, and a third capped player, Jamie Hall, was released. Salisbury moved to Surrey and all-rounder Danny Law, a player in whom Haynes had identified big potential, signed for Essex. Martin Speight, meanwhile, a gifted wicketkeeper-batsman, moved to Durham, where he would never fulfil his promise.

Matters were moving much faster off the field than on it. Tony 'Lester' Pigott, like Moores, was not born in Sussex. He was born in Fulham. But, as with Moores, Sussex never had a more devoted servant. Like Robin Marlar he was educated at Harrow, where Marlar once played cricket with Pigott's father, Tom. But Pigott junior was only two months old when the family moved to Sussex, and when he was 11 he managed to dissuade his father from making a move to Kent. Pigott came through from the Sussex Young Cricketers and broke into the first-class game in a sensational way: his first three wickets were a hat-trick. As a fast bowler, his run-up often looked faster than his delivery, but England trusted him with a Test cap when they ran out of players during a tour of New Zealand and he did not let them down.

Pigott, who three years earlier had been told that his career might be over after he was diagnosed with a double fracture of the vertebrae, had been playing state cricket in Wellington at the time of his call-up. Ian Botham wanted him to move to Somerset to form a new-ball attack with the great West Indian Joel Garner. But he pulled out of the move at the last minute. 'I couldn't bowl for Somerset like I bowl for Sussex,' he said afterwards. But Pigott had been a member of that devastated NatWest Final side in 1993, and three years later he was released by the county. He finished his playing career with Surrey and became second XI coach under David Gilbert, who had been brought in from the Australian Cricket Academy to be the club's cricket manager.

When Pigott spoke at a Sussex Cricket Society meeting in January 1997, he was surprised by the anger of members. 'Sussex had already lost five capped players, and another – Speight – was about to go. Sussex supporters weren't supposed to be fiery and passionate, but they were that night.'

When Pigott joined a number of supporters for a drink that night he met Jim May, who told him that he was going to stand for the committee. May told Pigott that as a former player with a higher profile he was in a good position to change things. Pigott, with the advice of a solicitor, collected signatures and called for an extraordinary general meeting, which was scheduled for 8 April. Aided by a public relations company, he had wind in his sails. That EGM never took place – the AGM in March settled everything.

By now Pigott, May and Marlar had joined forces. On the morning of the meeting Pigott remembers club chairman Ken Hopkins being '...blasé about the whole thing. He thought we would have the AGM and then the EGM and that everything would be sorted out. But it was a lot more serious than that. There was a definite momentum building.'

Peter Moores recalled: 'When I arrived, Tony's supporters were outside the Grand with Sussex 2000 leaflets. You could see that they had planned things well. The room was absolutely buzzing. I had never known an atmosphere like it. You just knew something momentous was going to happen.'

An already nervous club was further embarrassed when it was announced that secretary Nigel Bett would not be attending. The previous day the local newspaper, the *Brighton Argus*, had reproduced a picture taken by Bett's wife, Barbara, which had appeared in *British Naturism* magazine. Bett was on a nudist beach in the Canary Islands with only a black and white scarf covering his manhood. On the night the club was left feeling equally naked. Today, 11 years after the event, May, who is now the club's treasurer, recalled: 'The atmosphere that evening was absolutely electric. I moved a notice of motion which rejected the committee's report. That was the crucial moment. But we were all just tapping into the disillusionment of the members. Alan Caffyn deflected criticism by using the players as scapegoats. And Ken Hopkins must have been the shortest-serving chairman in the club's history – about two minutes.

'It has been an extraordinary journey. We just wanted to create the right culture, the right environment, for things to get better. The wheels had come off and we just wanted an improvement. Instead, everything has exceeded our wildest dreams, with the winning of not just one but three Championships.

'Robin was a very important figure in all of this. He has a very generous spirit. And, yes, he's right. It was my son, Kevin, who recorded him on TV fulminating about everything. That's when I contacted him – but I don't remember using the 'f' word!'

Pigott was appointed director of cricket and acting chief executive by Marlar, who was the new chairman. If Marlar thinks that May is the unsung hero, May feels that the now departed Pigott should get more credit than he is given these days. May, who likened events to the lifting of the Iron Curtain in Eastern Europe, said: 'Everyone knows that Tony was totally committed and had great passion. But it is sometimes forgotten that he also had a lot of vision.

'This was shown in a number of ways. First, he realised that we needed a new and charismatic leader to put down a marker for the club and show everyone else that we meant business.

'Secondly, he sold that vision to Chris Adams, a player who was being pursued by a number of counties. I know that we paid Chris a lot of money, but he did buy into the challenge and the vision that was placed before him. Lester was also the man who appointed Peter Moores as coach. And he was he man who said that we had to build floodlights. When Gilbert arrived he brought a bit more structure with him. But Tony had the vision in the first place.

'Peter also did a fantastic job here, and he knew it was a gamble to bring in Mushtaq Ahmed because there were some people who thought he might be over the hill.'

Former players John Snow and John Spencer, who had resigned from the previous comittee, were all Pigott supporters and now filled the empty seats in the new committee room. So did the energetic Don Trangmar, a former board director of Marks and Spencer. Another important name, with an eye to the way things would go, was Mark Robinson, who made his debut for the club that season along with Neil Taylor and Amar Khan. After a sequence of disappointing results, Marlar gave Pigott a bigger say in team selection, damaging the status of Haynes, who would soon be gone. The revolution had taken place, but the blood-letting was far from over.

When Pigott brought in his old boss, Gilbert, from Surrey, it was another feather in his cap. Little did he know that this particular recruitment would be the beginning of the end for him. Gilbert was appointed deputy chief executive and director of cricket in October 1997. He was given a two-year contract.

'Basically,' said Gilbert later, 'a structure did not exist. Tony was effectively serving two masters in Robin Marlar and Don Trangmar, who was playing a bigger role as vice-chairman, and a lot of the time it was a case of the tail wagging the dog.

'I remember going to a staff meeting just prior to my commencement, which was held in the staff room at Marks and Spencer in Worthing, of all places, and being shocked by how much people who were performing minor roles in the operation had to say about everything to do with the club. To be fair, Tony inherited an absolute mess. I was brought in to help him bring some structure to the place.'

Adam Tarrant was appointed as commercial manager but dismissed just six months later and replaced by Neil Lenham, who is still at the club. Marlar handed over the chairmanship to Trangmar, and Moores, replaced as captain by Adams, was now free from playing responsibilities and able to concentrate on his coaching duties. Trangmar and Gilbert soon bonded, further eroding Pigott's already vulnerable position. Gilbert said, 'You can't help but like Tony. He's a lovable rogue. But his spending was irrational and largely unaccountable, and I was getting increasingly fed up clearing up the wreckage.

'It was very unfair on Tony to give him a job for which he was entirely unsuited. He was always popular with the members and the committee because he always wore his heart on his sleeve as a player, giving absolutely everything, and then he was the catalyst for change when the club moved direction. But I felt that he was simply not up to the job.'

On 23 September 1999 it was announced that Pigott was leaving he club for 'personal reasons.' For a long time it had been clear that the responsibilities of Gilbert and Pigott were overlapping, that there was room for only one man and that the Australian was the more capable, for all Pigott's earlier inspirations.

Gilbert added: 'In the last weeks before Tony left we hardly spoke. Our relationship had deteriorated quite badly. That was a shame because we had been good friends and he was, after all, the person who created the position and brought me to the club.'

Pigott said: 'When Don took over as chairman and then David came in I felt a lot easier because I knew that if I was to be run over by a bus the future of the club was in the hands of two people who shared the same vision as me.

'From the moment I appointed him, David told me he didn't want the job of chief executive, but as time wore on I felt he was undermining me. I remember attending a meeting before the World Cup game at Hove. The Indian team manager couldn't believe I was chief executive. He thought David was, because in their dealings David hadn't told him otherwise.

'I told David that we had to work together for the good of Sussex cricket. A week later he offered to resign if we paid up the end of his contract, but I refused. I was always going to make mistakes, but I think we achieved a lot while I was there as well. I don't regret anything that happened. I think David felt guilty about what happened. Every time I came to the ground after that he would run a mile.'

Gilbert and Trangmar, who seemed to take responsibility for everything that happened at the club, worked well together. But at the end of July 2001, Gilbert told Sussex that he would leaving the club in order to return to his native New South Wales, where he would be chief executive. It was the job he had long coveted. It was also, perhaps, a timely departure, because he had not been seeing eye to eye with Moores, and after a disappointing season in 2000 there could have been more blood-letting had he not gone to Sydney.

Then, at the start of the 2002 season, Trangmar resigned as chairman amid mutterings from other committee members that he was too hands-on and autocratic. Trangmar was clearly upset by his sudden departure. 'If you haven't got the full support of everyone, what's the point of carrying on?' he shrugged. 'It was their decision to make the change but I was disappointed. They said I resigned for personal reasons, which was nice, but it wasn't true.'

Pigott was not at all surprised. 'That was always going to be the way with Don,' he said. 'That's the nature of the beast. I had felt more unsettled when Don was chairman because he wanted to make more decisions himself.'

Meanwhile, in a Sydney bar just outside the Sydney Cricket Ground in March 2008, Gilbert raised a glass to the Sussex success story, and toasted himself, too, in the autumn sunshine. New South Wales had just won the Pura Cup – Australia's championship – for the third time in six years, which is almost as impressive as Sussex's recent record.

'This is a proud moment for me, but also for Sussex,' he said. 'I went back to Hove last season and I look forward to doing so again soon in the near future. I had four years there and I do feel I made a contribution to what has happened in recent years. Good luck to them – and congratulations for having the vision to sign Mushtaq Ahmed, whose record of 450 wickets in five years is just awesome. It was a bit of a gamble to sign him, but what a brilliant move it was.'

This has been, then, the most eventful decade in the club's history. Heads rolled but then trophies came in. One day it would be nice to see Gilbert, Trangmar, Marlar, Moores and Pigott back at Hove together, sharing a glass in the pavilion. Nice, but not likely.

Chapter 8
Robbo

IT WAS little short of purgatory for everyone in the County Ground on that agonising Saturday afternoon in September 2007, while Sussex's Championship destiny was being decided at The Oval.

'One player described it as like waiting in hospital for the birth of his daughter,' recalled all-rounder Robin Martin-Jenkins, a veteran of all three titles. 'I thought it was more like a funeral wake for a close friend. No one could decide whether we should be laughing or crying.'

Some players hid in the dressing room, others, like Martin-Jenkins, found that the more time they spent in the jacuzzi, the more Lancashire wickets fell. Yet Mark Robinson felt more relaxed and calm than he had been at any point throughout the season: 'I was quite happy to bowl at my kids on the outfield and wait to see what happened. I knew we had done our best and that if Lancashire had beaten Surrey they would have deserved to win the Championship.'

They did not, of course, and it fell to Robinson to inform the dressing room when the last Lancashire wicket fell: 'I was on the phone to my parents in Hull, who were watching on TV when Cork got out. A few seconds later the place was bedlam.'

For the players, it did not take long before what they had pulled off began to sink in. But the process of evaluating Sussex's achievements since he succeeded Peter Moores as head coach in 2005 will take considerably longer for Robinson. A whole lifetime perhaps.

'One day I will look back and be really proud of the influence I have had during one of the most successful periods in the club's history,' he said. 'It will happen, but I might have my grandchildren on my knee when it does.'

'As a coach, you are always looking to the next challenge. You never stop thinking about what lies ahead, and that often means you are not really able to look back on what you have already achieved.'

For Robinson, that was definitely the scenario at the end of the 2007 season. 'The month after the season ends is one of the hardest times for a coach. You are settling contracts, organising budgets, talking to agents and planning pre-season. There are times when you just want everyone to leave you alone, but they won't. Players can get away from everything, but it's really hard for a coach.

'I'm not complaining, because I accept it as part of the job. You can't back away because you're tired. But there are times when you would like a bit more empathy with the position because it makes it hard to reflect on what you have achieved as an individual.'

When he succeeded Moores, few would have expected Robinson to have had a better record of success than his predecessor within just two years – back-to-back Championships and Sussex's first triumph in a Lord's one-day Final since 1986. Of course, he inherited a wonderful legacy when Moores went to work

Mark Robinson tucks in ahead of the C&G Trophy Final in August 2006.

for the ECB, but there was no guarantee that he could sustain it. What did help was that Robinson was already held in as high regard in the dressing room and at the club itself as Moores had been. He joined Sussex as a player when they were at their lowest ebb in the wake of the 1997 'revolution' and played his part in establishing Sussex as a First Division county. Chris Adams maintains that he always felt more confident when he was leading out a side with the ultra-reliable Robinson in his bowling attack.

When Robinson turned to coaching in 2003, initially with the second team, comparisons with his old boss were inevitable. Both had established their reputation in coaching after solid, if unspectacular, playing careers. 'Not only that, but people thought we were similar because we were both northerners, which was a ridiculous thing to base an assumption on,' said Robinson.

Having worked as part of Moores's coaching team for three years, the succession, on the face of it at least, looked a seamless one, but for Robinson the reality was different. 'When I took over as coach I was worried, scared even. It was intimidating watching how Pete operated. He could switch from one subject, be it a player's contract, to another, say the latest theory on fast bowling, so comfortably.

'But then I found myself in charge and suddenly you are doing exactly the same things, albeit in a slightly different style. Like most things, when you are doing it you find yourself with less time to think and sometimes you're flying by the seat of your pants, making mistakes but doing other things well.

'He was a hard act to follow, of course he was, and I definitely approach certain things differently to Pete. What has helped us continue the success is that when I took over the continuity at the club remained.'

That is the key. Like Moores before him, Robinson has a hardworking, loyal team of coaches under him in Mark Davis, who runs the second team, and Academy director Keith Greenfield. And until his retirement at the end of last season there was Les Lenham, who has been a fixture at Hove for more than 50 years as player, coach and trusted confidant of many batsmen.

'I have fantastic back-up from the coaches I work with. Mark and Keith are absolute rocks. I sometimes wonder whether people appreciate just how much all three of us go up and down the various squads, working with players in the Academy right up to the first team. There are certain jobs I can delegate to them, but because we are a small coaching staff at a small county we all have to multi-task massively.'

Then there is perhaps the most important relationship of all, that between coach and captain.

'You would go over the top in the trenches for someone like Chris Adams. He was the best captain I played under, and our relationship now gets better every year.'

* * * * *

Being coached by a Yorkshire legend like Ray Illingworth must have been the best feeling in the world for a cricket-mad 14-year-old desperate to play for his native county. But Mark Robinson was nearly lost to the game in those formative years.

'My memories of that time are not good,' he recalls. 'Yorkshire had a very good scouting system in those days, and I was invited to nets in the old Winter Shed at Headingley. My contemporaries included Darren Gough, Martyn Moxon and Rob Andrew, who made his name as an outstanding England rugby player, of course.

'Illy was one of the coaches, and so was Doug Padgett, who played more than 500 games for Yorkshire. But I lived in Hull, so it was a 120-mile round trip every time, and I hated it. The atmosphere was cold and unfriendly, and I just never felt that I fitted in. But my own determination and the support of my parents kept me going.'

Robinson played representative cricket for Humberside, Yorkshire and the North at Under-15s and for England Under-19s. He made his Yorkshire second-team debut as a 17-year-old against Northamptonshire in July 1983, where his teammates included David Byas, Richard Blakey and Ashley Metcalfe, all of whom would have long careers with the county. He bowled 22 wicket-less overs but did score 17 not out – batting at number nine. The name M.A. Robinson did not appear that high on a scorecard too often after that.

Yorkshire, their fast-bowling resources well stocked, were prepared to give Robinson a one-year contract after his A-levels but, as he mulled over their offer, Northamptonshire came in.

Mark Robinson appeals vociferously.

'Northants had a very good scout in the North East called Brian Reynolds, who picked up the likes of David Ripley and Alan Walker,' remembered Robinson. 'I was all set to go to Trent Polytechnic to do a teacher-training course, but Northants offered me a two-year contract in 1986 and it proved to be a great move.'

His first-class debut came in July 1987 against Lancashire. His first victim was Steve O'Shaughnessy, his second Mike Watkinson. Two decades later he would again lock horns with Watkinson, when they were the respective coaches of the top two teams in the country.

'They were great days, and I loved every minute. Northants put me in digs with a wonderful couple called Terry and Pat Evans and they became like my second mum and dad. There weren't many local players in the side, but we all seemed to get on.

'I'll never forget that first game against Lancashire. I even remember my first first-class runs off Patrick Patterson, who was a fearsome West Indian fast bowler. I got a couple first ball with a tickle down the leg-side. It was all downhill after that with the bat though!'

Between 1987 and 1991 Robinson played in 59 first-class games for Northamptonshire, taking 136 wickets. He was also a regular in their one-day side and someone skipper Allan Lamb relied on to bowl the crucial final overs.

'Two one-day games for Northants still stick in my mind. In the 1990 NatWest Trophy I bowled the last over against Worcestershire in the quarter-final when Ian Botham was on strike on 82 not out and they needed eight to win. But I restricted Botham to just four, and we won by four runs.

'In the semi-final, against Hampshire, Lamby screwed up the overs and I had to bowl the last over, but fortunately I got P.J. Bakker and Raj Maru out, and we were in the Final. Unfortunately, we lost the toss against Lancashire in the days when the Final started at 10.30am in

Surely that's out? Mark Robinson in appealing mood against Yorkshire in September 1998.

early September, and batting first was a nightmare. By 11.30am we were 39–5. I took 1–26 (and scored three not out), but we were well beaten.'

Robinson regularly shared the new ball in the Championship with West Indian legend Curtly Ambrose, and contemporaries remember him as a player who never shirked responsibility. Nick Cook, who played at Northampton between 1986 and 1994, said: 'Robbo was part of a stronghold of Yorkshiremen at the club, and I loved playing with him and the likes of David Ripley and Alan Walker because they were the backbone of county sides, the unsung heroes.

'His partnership with Curtly Ambrose worked well, despite Mark moaning that he always had to bowl uphill into the wind. Those two performances when we reached the 1990 NatWest Final were match-winning ones.

'It was no surprise to me when he went into coaching. He was always eager to embrace modern ideas and technology, but he still has traditional views and a passion for the game.'

'That was a golden era for county cricket,' said Robinson. 'Things weren't quite as professional as they are now, and it was a very sociable game, even at that level. I enjoyed my whole career, but my period with Northants was a special time.'

It was a surprise, therefore, certainly at Northampton, when Robinson rejoined Yorkshire in 1991. The lure of representing the county of his birth proved too strong.

'It wasn't hard to go back. All Yorkshiremen want to play for their home county, and I was missing my family. Steve Oldham was coach, and he signed me, but in my first season I struggled. The players weren't as close a bunch as Northants were, but that helped toughen me up, and in my second year I never looked back.'

His finest hour as a professional cricketer came in July 1993 against his former county on a damp wicket at Harrogate when he took a career-best 9–36. Yet the story could have been totally different, according to Rob Bailey, a teammate of Robinson's at Northamptonshire.

'When we arrived on the second morning [there was no play on the first day] we found that rain had seeped under the covers and the biggest puddle was on a length at one end. We lost the toss, but Paul Jarvis only bowled three overs before pulling a muscle and returning to the dressing room. That injury changed the course of the game.

'Robbo came into the attack and put ball after ball in the centre of that wet patch. Our captain Allan Lamb blamed poor technique, but Robbo was unplayable on the day. We were all out for 97, but Peter Hartley denied Robbo the chance of getting all 10 wickets when he got Lamby out.'

Bailey top-scored with 68 when Northants followed-on, and Robinson picked up three more wickets for a match return of 12–124, also a career best.

'I can still picture the reaction of the Harrogate crowd now,' said David Ripley, once a teammate but now one of Robinson's nine victims. 'They clapped him all the way as he went for a walk around the ground.'

For the next two years Robinson was a key member of the Yorkshire attack. He played in front of 21,000 at Headingley in a NatWest Trophy quarter-final against Lancashire in 1995, with another 2,000 locked out, but when Martyn Moxon was replaced by David Byas as captain for the 1996 season he abruptly found himself out in the cold.

'Byas never rated me – it's as simple as that. Before 1996 I'd had a great time. I was playing for my home county and a lot of good young bowlers were emerging at Yorkshire, including Darren Gough, Matthew Hoggard and Alex Wharf, all of whom went on to play for their country. They were all pressing for a place, and in 1996 I never got a look in.'

Robinson played all his cricket that year in Yorkshire's second team. For someone who had been a key member of the first-team attack for the previous five seasons, pitching up at places like Todmorden, Worksop, Rocester, Bingley and Castleford must have been soul-destroying. But he still bowled as if it were a Test match, finished with 37 wickets and was a virtual ever-present.

But he also knew that at the end of the season he would not be kept on. Bailey was keen to take him back to Northamptonshire: 'I was captain by then and keen to re-sign him. Unfortunately, and I still don't know why, those in higher positions did not agree.'

Glamorgan also expressed an interest, but did not follow it up, and by March 1997, when he should have been preparing for the new season, it appeared Robinson's future lay outside the first-class game, even though, at 31, he knew he still had something to offer.

Then came the phone call which was to change the course of his career.

'Jason Lewry had just gone bust with the back injury which was to keep him out for the season and Sussex had already lost five of their best players. Peter Moores gave me a ring. I went down to Hove, met Pete and from the first day it felt right. The club had been stripped bare by all that had happened on and off the field, and it was a fantastic opportunity to be part of the rebuilding which was going on.

'Fortunately Peter and some of the senior pros who were left – guys like Neil Lenham,

Mark Robinson bowls against Surrey in August 1999.

Bill Athey, Keith Greenfield and Neil Taylor, whom we signed from Kent, stood for the same things as me: loyalty, hard work and respect for the game and everyone at the club, from the chairman down to the cleaner.'

Robinson never looked back after an unforgettable debut against one of his former counties, Northamptonshire, at Hove in April 1997, when he took 6–78. Moores knew what he was getting from his new signing and quickly dubbed him the 'Angus Fraser of the South Coast.'

'He was a wicketkeeper's dream. He had the ability to make the ball spit and bounce off the seam and put batsmen under pressure. I think he had realised that he wasn't Dennis Lillee [briefly, a Northamptonshire teammate], and he agreed to let me stand up to him.

'He snarled and growled a bit about that decision, but it was his accuracy and consistency that eventually undid the best of batsmen. His line and length were impeccable and because he hit the seam more often than not from a high action, he was always asking questions of batsmen – you always felt you were in the game when Robbo was bowling.

'Even after he retired I still found myself looking at pitches and thinking "Robbo would have bowled well on that."'

Sussex finished bottom of the pile in Robinson's first season at Hove, but reinforcements arrived the following year in the shape of Chris Adams and Michael Bevan as overseas player, and slowly the county's fortunes improved.

'I knew Robbo was a fine bowler, but I had no idea how good he was, not just at managing his own situation, but also as leader of a reputable attack,' said Adams. 'Robbo was a captain's dream. You could throw him the ball in any conditions and ask him to deliver a tight spell, usually up the hill, and nine times out of 10 he would deliver, with a couple of wickets nearly always thrown in.'

Robinson was also a terrific help to Sussex's emerging bowlers, Jason Lewry and James Kirtley, and a key member of what became a happy dressing room again.

'I remember sitting relatively unnoticed in the ground the day he made his debut against Northants,' said Lewry. 'I heard a lot of comments ranging from 'Why have we signed this bloke?' to 'That's the longest run-up I have ever seen.' But after he took those six wickets, I think those were the last negative things anyone said about him at Sussex.

'He was a truly inspired signing. He is a man you would want on your side: a fierce competitor, a team man and ultra-consistent.'

Another teammate, Tony Cottey, remembered Robinson as 'the most dedicated and professional player I had the privilege to play with in 18 years in the game.'

'Robbo and I were housemates for two of my seasons at Hove and great times they were, too. He was also the hub of the dressing room, organising all the team meals, fines and drinking games (on days off, of course) in his role as social chairman.'

It would have perhaps been fitting had Robinson ended his career with a Championship-winner's medal. But a year before Sussex lifted the first title in their history, he retired. In 2001 he had finished with 57 wickets in the Championship as Sussex gained promotion to Division One, but the following year he played in just one four-day game and a handful of one-day matches. Mind you, he made his mark in that solitary Championship appearance against Yorkshire at Arundel, surviving for 11 balls at the end to ensure his side drew the match. He played his last game for Sussex on 15 September 2002 against Derbyshire in the one-day League, departing to a standing ovation from the Hove crowd.

In 74 first-class games for Sussex he had taken 215 wickets at a miserly average of 26.73, the best of his career. He was also a regular in their one-day team, with 120 wickets, and helped Sussex win the Second Division of the one-day League in 1999, the county's first silverware for 13 years.

Robinson never won international recognition and was seldom mentioned as a potential England player, even in an era when plenty of bowlers with worse records than him played for their country. But he was fortunate to play with some outstanding talent. At Yorkshire there was Sachin Tendulkar, the county's first overseas player, and then at Northamptonshire three outstanding fast bowlers: Dennis Lillee, Curtly Ambrose and the fiery West Indian Winston Davis. 'Winston took me under his wing in my early days there,' said Robinson.

His XI of English teammates would include nine players who represented their country: Martyn Moxon, Wayne Larkins, Michael Vaughan, Allan Lamb, Chris Adams, David Capel, Nick Cook, Darren Gough and James Kirtley.

Robinson would proudly make up the XI in that team, but which opponents caused him most problems? 'I always struggled against small batsmen for some reason. Paul Johnson, of Nottinghamshire, always used to score runs against me because he judged length really quickly. Of all the players I came up against, he was my nemesis.

'When I was batting I always used to think Lancashire's Wasim Akram could hit me anywhere from my ankle to my head and every part in between at will! And I never used to like facing Anil Kumble – I couldn't even slog him properly.'

No appreciation of Robinson's career is complete without mention of that modest record with the bat. He holds a unique place in the record books after taking his 500th first-class wicket (he finished with 584) and scoring his 500th run in the same game. But after those heady early days at number nine in the Yorkshire second-team order, Robinson found a permanent home at number 11. He once went 11 successive innings without scoring a run, although in fairness seven of those were nought not outs, but even his batting improved at Hove, where he worked as hard as any of the bowlers to improve his record. His Sussex average of 5.14 was considerably better than his career average of 4.01.

* * * * *

The next phase of Mark Robinson's career soon took shape. In 2002 he succeeded Keith Greenfield as second-team coach when Greenfield was appointed the club's first Academy Director, a job Robinson had applied for himself.

'I had been coaching at my Academy in Hull, which I'd set up when I played for Yorkshire, for a long time and knew it was something I wanted to develop when I stopped playing because I have always coached.'

The job meant a major domestic upheaval for his wife Julia, whom he had married in 1994, four years after they met, and their two young children, who continued to be based in Hull when he was playing for Sussex. 'It wasn't really an option,' said Julia. 'Coaching Sussex was a dream job for Mark.'

Although Robinson was second-team coach first and foremost, Moores had made sure he was involved in as many aspects of the first team as possible. When the seconds were not playing he would be in the nets or organising warm-ups. 'Pete was brilliant to me,' said Robinson. 'He always kept me involved and made me feel part of the success we had under him, it was one of his strengths.'

There was never any doubt about who would succeed Moores when he took up his new role at the ECB National Academy at Loughborough at the end of the 2005 season. Robinson was doing an excellent job with the second team and guided them to the one-day trophy in August 2005 with victory over Nottinghamshire at Horsham.

'It was great because, although I was often involved in the first team, I had my own side to manage and look after as well, and we had a bit of success, which is always nice.'

And if the club had any misgivings about promoting him, Moores gave him a glowing recommendation on his last day in the job as Sussex clinched promotion back to the First Division of the National League as champions following victory over Yorkshire at Hove.

'I knew the coaching at the club was in great hands,' said Moores. 'But I also knew that Robbo was his own man, who would stamp his own personality on the team.'

Their coaching methods are similar, and both value the traditions and integrity of the game. One difference is the way they cope with the stresses and strains of a normal season.

'The job is your life, it's all consuming. You take it home, you take it on holiday and you take it with you when you go to the supermarket,' said Robinson. 'On a typical day during the season it can be so consuming that you have trouble sleeping. It is hard to switch off. Once I'm awake that's it, I get up, even if it's 4am. I'm quite good at vegetating, I can happily sit in front of the TV (he is an avid fan of the soaps) or watch *Sky Sports News* and think of nothing, but Pete's release would be the gym. I'll quite happily watch a repeat of *Coronation Street* while Pete will go and row for 5,000 metres or run on the treadmill for half an hour.'

Neither man feels comfortable in the spotlight, although they are both media-friendly. It was typical of Moores that when Sussex clinched the Championship for the first time in 2003 he was not pictured in any of the celebratory photographs, despite cajoling from his players. He preferred to let them bask in the glory. Robinson is the same.

Mark Robinson, Chris Adams and Peter Moores try to keep warm during the pre-season photo-call at Hove in 2004.

Moores, with no little help from Chris Adams of course, will always be credited with turning Sussex from perennial under-achievers to a team of winners. Yet in the two seasons since he succeeded him Robinson has already won more trophies. It might give some people an inferiority complex. So does Robinson feel in any way undervalued?

'Perhaps,' he says. 'We all like praise, and I am no different from anyone else in that regard. In terms of recognising what I have helped Sussex achieve I know I have played a part, firstly as a player and now as a coach. It is up to others to judge what that contribution has been.'

What about his personal ambitions? Moores seemed earmarked for greater things before Sussex won their first Championship, as his innovative methods, and the way he embraced new technology, were shamelessly copied by other counties and got him noticed at international level. Robinson's record gives him every right to be regarded as one of the best coaches in the country at the moment, but when the next big job in English cricket becomes available you could not say with total certainty that he would be thought of as a leading contender.

Mark Robinson shows off the brochure that promoted his testimonial in 2005.

'I am quite modest, but I think I am good at what I do – I make teams work,' he said. Which is probably as close as you are going to get to Robinson blowing his own trumpet. He is also a great believer that outside factors will determine his own future and that of his county.

'All county coaches have different problems and challenges. At Lancashire, for instance, Mike Watkinson has had to cope with having a lot of international players for a long time. It is something Pete Moores didn't have, but Chris Adams and I had it in 2007, and it is quite hard work because you are dealing with egos, whether it's building up guys who have not done well for England or getting guys who suddenly think they are the bees-knees back on track.

'But money is my biggest fear. The market for players is getting stupid, and I worry that one day we will not have the money to compete, to keep our best players and sign new ones. That is the reality for most small counties.'

During the summer, pure coaching is what he does least. There simply is not time to spend two or three hours with a player working on technical problems. Even when the team are not playing, there is paperwork to catch up on and Academy and second-team players to watch.

'I have coached for a long time now, but I would say that I prefer playing. I do love coaching, and in the winter I'm more of a proper coach than in the summer, when I see myself more as team manager.'

Robin Martin-Jenkins regards him as equally adept at man-management as coach. A good example of that came in May 2007 when Mushtaq Ahmed, still struggling desperately to come to terms with the death of Pakistan coach Bob Woolmer, was openly talking about retirement. Not at the end of the season, but just a month into it.

'I met Mushy for a coffee down the road from the ground to basically give him a telling off, which is not something I ever expected to have to do to him. All I had heard from him for weeks was that he wanted to retire, and that he was missing his family too much. A lot of it was a reaction to Bob Woolmer's death. I just asked him "Is this how you want your career to end?" The more he had talked about it the worse he had played and the more disgruntled he was as a person. We had a chat and it worked, and we all know how well Mushy did for the rest of the season.

A pensive Mark Robinson watches Sussex suffer against Surrey at Hove in May 2007.

Chris Adams on the attack. Adams has forged a terrific partnership with Robinson.

'When things you do like that don't come off, it's never a waste of time because at least you have the experience behind you when a similar situation crops up. It's one aspect of the job which is often undervalued. Where is something like that reflected in the averages or the playing record? But when it works, as that did, it can give you as much satisfaction as any victory on the field.'

It is unlikely Robinson will ever lose his Yorkshire accent, but he regards Sussex as his home now, although trips back home to see family and watch his beloved Hull City are still treasured. Who knows what the future holds for Sussex under him? The only certainty is that a new era in the county's history is not far away. By the end of 2009 the county could have seen the last of Mushtaq Ahmed and Chris Adams, and perhaps Murray Goodwin as well. Few outside Hove would rate Sussex's chances of maintaining their status as the best side in the country without that trio.

'Things will change, and we might not be as successful as we have been, but I have to believe that we will get things in place to make the success continue,' he said. 'I think we have been successful with Chris, Mushy and Murray – not because of them. What we do have now is a very good core of players. It's a bit like the spine in a football team.

'If you look at Australia as an example, in the past year they have lost the best spin bowler the world has ever seen in Shane Warne, one of the best fast bowlers ever in Glenn McGrath and the best wicketkeeper-batsman in Adam Gilchrist, yet they are still comfortably the best team in the world. They have found ways of winning games in other ways.

'Don't get me wrong – Chris and Mushy have played a massively important role, but things that are built to last are not built around one or two people. Chris has given us inspiration, stability and leadership in the same way as Peter Moores did, but when I took over things didn't fall apart and it will be the same when a new captain takes over from Chris.

'When Mushtaq goes we will have to win games in other ways, as we did without him in the past. In the 1980s Essex dominated county cricket without a world-class spinner, and Warwickshire's success in the 1990s was built around Allan Donald, so it does happen.'

Whoever the personnel are, Robinson will continue to bring the same honesty and values to his role that he always has. It's an ethos he will always strive to protect.

'Perhaps the thing I have done best as a coach is understand what this club is about. I love it when outsiders talk about us and as if there is some sort of mythology as to how we have achieved our success, even if the reality is not quite the same.

'I am with people at this club who share my beliefs and principles. It is a magnificent place to work as a result of that, and all the time I am with Sussex I will make sure those values remain. Who knows? It could be my downfall in the end – I will probably fall on my sword because I have been too outspoken in defending something I believe in.'

Chapter 9
The Coach's Coach

THERE is a sombre moment in that most melodramatic of George Cukor's films, *A Star Is Born*, when James Mason walks into the sea and is never seen again. Anyone who ventured down to the Hove seafront in the pre-season of 1998 may have thought that Sussex, who had finished bottom of the table the previous summer under the captaincy of Peter Moores, had agreed upon a suicide pact.

Chris Adams, the Sussex captain, takes up the story: 'On the first day of pre-season everyone gathered, from our overseas player, Michael Bevan, to the youngest pro. "Follow me," said Peter, who headed off in the direction of the seafront with a motley assortment of players behind him.

'He strung us out in a line on the beach and told us to walk slowly and deliberately into the water until it came up to our necks, turn around and walk back again.

'It was late March, the water was freezing and all we were allowed to wear were our shorts. The boys didn't know what to think, but when they saw that Peter was going to take part as well they didn't really have a choice.

'It turned out to be a master stroke in terms of getting the squad to operate together. It was a simple but effective way of improving team spirit insomuch as it provided a talking point for the whole squad during those difficult first few days of pre-season, particularly for new players trying to integrate with the senior men.'

Moores had been appointed coach for that season, and this was the first of many original moves. Sussex finished seventh in the Championship in 1998 to qualify for the new Super Cup and Tony Pigott, the club's chief executive, who had appointed his good friend, said 'I couldn't have hoped for better than that. If someone had told me at the end of 1997 that we would come seventh the following summer, I would have laughed. We had had a difficult time the year before, to put it mildly, so this felt like a great achievement.'

There are few people in cricket who know the England coach better than Pigott, though by the time Moores and captain Chris Adams had landed the club's first Championship in 2003 he had left the club.

'Peter and I became very close friends. We got to know each other very well when we were players. He is probably the only person who could have led Sussex through a lot of changes while keeping a very positive and enthusiastic attitude. His motivation and general management of the cricket side were outstanding.

'The phrase "model professional" is used too often and has become demeaned as a result, but that's really what he is. I roomed with him for 10 years and just knew he was the right man for the job.

'His enthusiasm is his main strength, the thing that really strikes you when you first meet him. But there is so much more to him than that. His man-management is also very strong. He analyses a game very well and strives to create the right environment. And he just knows the game so well. When England appointed him national coach in 2007 he was absolutely the right man for the job.'

The England and Wales Cricket Board appointed Moores in April 2007 and did not even bother to interview the other favourite for the job, Tom Moody, who had done an impressive job with Sri Lanka, not least in their encounters with England, but was now available for a new challenge. They did not talk to Dav Whatmore either, another international coach who had done much good work with Bangladesh but who had announced his intention to stand down at the end of May. John Wright, a former India coach, was another who was overlooked. Bob Woolmer (South Africa), John Bracewell (New Zealand) and Mickey Arthur (South Africa) were also coming to the end of their contracts and beginning to think about fresh challenges.

After seven years as Sussex coach and another two as National Academy director in Loughborough, the ECB had seen enough and identified their man in advance. Moores was appointed less than 24 hours after Duncan Fletcher announced he would be standing down after England's last game in the World Cup in the West Indies. Eager, spruce, head-boyish, Moores today is the man charged with shaping the destiny of English cricket. Those who do not know him are a little surprised by his swift ascendancy, and some have even suggested that he is lightweight. They ask if enthusiasm is all he brings to the task. Those who do know him are generally convinced by the man and his methods. And no one knows him better than the people of Sussex, whose club he piloted to their first Championship in 164 years five years ago.

Moores was the Sussex coach when they won that sacred first title in 2003, and when he left two years later his legacy was no less important than the millions left to the club by elusive former president Spen Cama, who died in 2001. The difference is that Moores's inheritance, unlike Cama's money, has not caught the eye of the Revenue and Customs Capital Taxes Office. Moores proved to be one of the most original of cricket thinkers. Ten years ago the laptop coach had not yet arrived, but Moores already had organisational skills and an eye for detail that bordered on the forensic. He asked Rob Boddie, the county's librarian, to thumb through dog-eared Wisdens to discover which grounds favoured spin and which seam.

Gus Fraser, who now observes Moores as cricket correspondent of *The Independent*, first got to know Moores when they played against each other. He said: 'Peter was not a star performer, but he was a gutsy fighter who made the most of his ability. When he became coach in 1998 he quickly began to impress.

'When Middlesex played Sussex I used to look on in envy at the way they were drilled by Moores. Under his guidance, Sussex's practice sessions, warm-up drills and fielding routines before the start of play were slick and effective.

'Every player seemed to know what he was doing and they made us look like a disorganised group of raggy-arsed rangers. He was one of the first coaches to video each day's play, too.

Flag day. Chris Adams leads the celebrations for Sussex's first Championship in 2003.

Sussex also had debriefing sessions at the end of play, as I found out once when I stuck my head round their dressing-room door to see if any of them were coming down the pub for a quick pint. A day playing against Sussex made me realise why they were competing for trophies and we were not.'

But Moores is no anorak. He can sink the beer (and the red wine) with the best of them, and when he does he can erupt into song, for he was the team crooner in his playing days.

'*The Leader of the Pack* was always one of "Stiggsy's" favourites when we had a bit of a sing-song,' said his friend and former teammate Alan Wells, whose departure in 1997 led to Moores's appointment as captain. His party piece was *Wild Rover*, and he has also been known – with some lubrication – to work his way through the Elvis Presley songbook.

He has the ability to inspire. Mark Robinson, who succeeded him as coach at Hove, said: 'When I was a player I felt like going on a three-mile run every time I talked to Peter. He has that vital ability to lift people, to make them believe in themselves.'

So we are talking about quite a package here. He has, it seems, the ability to motivate, organise, man-manage and innovate. It is his misfortune, though he would never say so, to take charge of an England side that has been in steep decline over the previous two years. England peaked for the 2005 Ashes, but the cornerstone of that success, the four-pronged pace attack of Steve Harmison, Andrew Flintoff, Simon Jones and Matthew Hoggard, soon fell apart. By the time Moores took over, some serious rebuilding was required. And he could not fall back on the considerable services of Flintoff, who had proved himself to be the outstanding all-rounder in the world and given the side essential balance.

Anyone who saw the schoolboy Moores building up his strength and fitness with home-made dumbbells made out of old detergent bottles filled with sand knew, even before Pigott, that there was something special about him. He grew up with four brothers and three sisters in a three-storey townhouse in Macclesfield. He and his brothers, Tony, Stephen, James and Robert, played football and rugby with large stuffed mice.

'There were great Test matches, usually between England and the West Indies,' recalled Stephen. 'For a pitch we used a 20ft-long backyard and entry.'

The young Moores had the best inspiration there was. Alan Knott, considered by many to be England's greatest wicketkeeper, had written a book about his craft, and it was presented to Peter on his 12th birthday. It changed his life. Ultimately, that gift would shape the course of English cricket. Knott, now 62 and living in the Greek Islands, is an eccentric. He was England's gnomish, pointy-chinned Mr Punch behind the stumps. He could drive teammates crazy with his calisthenics and – for in his day hotel rooms were shared – by getting up very early in the morning.

When he toured the West Indies with England in 1973–74 he shared with Chris Old. Old told Knott that he did not want him waking him up by arising in the early hours. Knott told Old that he did not want him waking him up by getting back to the hotel late. 'We got on fine,' said Old. 'He was always up before I got back to the room!'

Knott was also a thoroughly unconventional batsman, though one who scored more than 4,000 runs for England in Tests, including five centuries. Knott was the great cricketer Moores, for all his efforts, would never become. As a cricketer, though, both behind and in front of the wicket, Moores could not have had a better role model.

'I know it sounds daft, but that book by Knotty really got me started,' said Moores. 'It was a big influence on my career. Knotty was a hero of every young cricketer at the time. And cricket was no longer a game but a way of life for me. I had made my mind up.'

Ian Wilson was his cricket master at Macclesfield's King Edward School. He said: 'I first saw him play in 1977 when he was a very small wicketkeeper-batsman in the Under-14 side. As cricket master I had gone along to watch him play in the Cheshire Schools' Cup Final. We won, and I remember a cover-drive to a very long boundary which had quality written all over it.

'This was really the last age-group cricket that Pete played at school as I brought him straight into the first XI. He was with a lot of older lads, and it was amazing how quickly he was accepted. That was not just because of his ability – and he was a cracking 'keeper who would stand up to the seamers, which was rare – but also because he was a genuine cricket-mad "character".

'We had this very close-knit group of working-class boys, with a huge group of dads who would follow them everywhere, and for an independent school that was very unusual. As a youngster joining a group of older kids to play serious cricket, Peter really had to be special, and he was.

'He was only half the size of the other boys, and his voice hadn't broken. When he appealed there was this huge, noisy squeak which the other lads really took to their hearts.

'He was captain in his final year. He was an absolutely natural leader, through example as well as tactics, for he had a pretty good coverage of tactics for a boy. They would have done anything for him.

'I thought he would play for England, as much for his attitude, his liveliness and enthusiasm, as his ability. He was really outstanding.'

At that level, his ability stood out. But what is more interesting is that Wilson was more impressed by the boy's approach to the game than any innate gifts behind the stumps.

'He always played hard but fair. He showed amazing dedication and stamina. During the school's annual post-exams cricket fortnight, when he was often on the field for virtually the whole game, day after day, he still managed to fit in his self-imposed daily session on his homemade training set-up. And he was always keen to learn and to talk cricket.

'It is the last characteristic which I have found the most striking over the years. The stories circulate of the cynicism of the county pros over the years – of how they are mercenaries interested only in playing-mediocrity and the next contract, of their lack of interest in post-match cricket chat at the bar.

'They are not true as far as Peter is concerned. I have met him from time to time for a beer over the years, and he has shown the same enthusiasm for the game and all that surrounds it that he did when he first played at school. But now he has taught me a lot more about coaching than I ever taught him.'

Late in the 1981 season King Edward's School played the MCC and Moores had a good game. He said: 'Freddie Millet did a lot of schools cricket in Macclesfield and always ran the MCC game. He was quite impressed and took me down to Lord's for a trial at the end of 1981. It went well, and they took me on.'

He played for England Schoolboys under the captaincy of his future boss Hugh Morris and joined the Lord's groundstaff in 1982. It was the year after former groundstaff boy Botham's Ashes and Don Wilson, the coach in those days, would cry: 'Just look what Botham did. That could be you!' Here, Moores, who was paid £32 every Friday afternoon, met Dermot Reeve, with whom he would share a dressing room, briefly, at Sussex before the latter's move to Warwickshire.

Reeve said: 'We were both about 18 at the time. And my strongest memory of Peter is of him practising even when the light had faded. Don Wilson had told everyone to get off and have a shower. Most of the boys could hardly walk by the end of the day and were counting the minutes to the final whistle. But when it came, Peter would carry on, full of enthusiasm. We called him Action Man Moores. And Peter made sure the coach's beer glass was never empty in the evening while he still had stories to tell.

'We were also expected to help sell scorecards, and I will always remember Peter handing them out with the same bubbly keenness that he had for the game. He was signed by Worcestershire halfway through my first year at Lord's, and I lost touch, for the time being, with a good friend whose attitude I admired greatly.'

Moores went to Worcestershire in 1982, some years before the Hick-Botham-Dilley inspired successes at the end of that decade. Worcestershire already had a regular keeper in David Humphries, but his understudy, Mark Vaughan, had broken his nose.

Moores said: 'I had one trial game, and they took me on for the rest of the season.' He played for the second XI, who won their Championship for the first time in 20 years. His captain was often Vanburn Holder, the West Indies fast bowler who is now one of the game's most experienced umpires.

'I wouldn't say he was the greatest of 'keepers,' said Holder, stroking his chin with tender wisdom. 'But he wasn't bad. He was always keen to play. He worked hard and wanted to learn everything. When the game was over he was happy to listen to cricket stories.'

One of his closest friends was Richard Illingworth, the Worcester slow left-arm. The pair shared digs for three years.

Illingworth recalls: 'We came under the watchful eye of the coach, Basil d'Oliveira. Off the field, we shared accommodation, travelled to away games in clapped-out cars and visited the nightclubs of Worcester. We were young, free and single in those days. We worked hard and played hard. They were great days, and they are now very happy memories.

'Pete was a good cook, I remember that. And he drove an old Allegro. I had a Hillman Avenger in those days, and we talked about driving better cars one day. We were good mates but very competitive against each other in practice games. He used to try to hit me as hard as the young Graeme Hick did when we got in the nets.'

Moores made his first-class debut for Worcestershire in 1983, against Somerset. He remembers flat-batting his first ball, from Ian Botham, through the covers for four and getting out next ball. He made seven appearances for the county that year and another four the following year.

But there was no future for Moores at New Road. By then the county had decided that Steve Rhodes, from Yorkshire, would be the long-term replacement for Humphries. Moores was released at the end of the 1984 season, but there were warm letters of recommendation from the county and Sussex offered him a trial the following March.

He was only 22, but there was already a coach stirring inside him. In the winter of 1984–85 he went to Zimbabwe. He played for Harare Sports Club, but coached at a college up the road.

'It was a tough introduction because of the amount of coaching I had to do. The following winter I coached Free State Country in South Africa. That was a very good standard.

'Even the club team I played for at weekends had eight or nine players with first-class experience. They were no Western Province, but it was still a heavy-duty job for someone who was 20-plus and still wet behind the ears.'

Ian Gould, who had joined Sussex from Middlesex in 1981 and won his cap the same year, was the established wicketkeeper-batsman at Hove when Moores moved there. Moores played just one match for Sussex in 1985, against Gloucestershire at Bristol in June, and then almost lost his career because of a serious back injury.

'The season of 1986 was basically a write-off,' he said. 'I had a series of injections. I remember seeing a doctor in Hastings just before Christmas. He gave me my last injection, and I remember thinking that was it, my career was over. He told me that if I was to have any chance of playing again I would have to swim 50 lengths every day before the start of the season.

'I had to be very disciplined in my rehabilitation, but I didn't mind that. In fact I loved it. I got really fit and never suffered from a bad injury again.'

In 1987 Gould was the Sussex captain, and sometimes he played as a batsman while Moores kept wicket. When Paul Parker and John Barclay went on to captain the club, Moores suddenly discovered that he was looked upon as one of the senior men in the team.

'John made a good impression on me pretty much straight after I got into the side. I remember an incident in my third or fourth game. Imran Khan had only been bowling for three overs with the new ball when John sidled up to me at the end of an over and asked me whether I thought he should take him off.

'I couldn't believe it. Here was the captain asking me whether we should replace someone who, at the time, was one of the best bowlers in the world. I couldn't answer him. I was speechless. But that day I vowed that when anyone asked for my thoughts on the game I would give them.'

Before long Moores would be the one asking for advice. He was made captain in 1997, when he succeeded Alan Wells. But it was a difficult year. Six capped players, including Wells, had left the club, and in a bitter, unpleasant atmosphere two wooden spoons were gathered in, in the Championship and the Sunday League. In the Benson and Hedges Cup, meanwhile, they lost to British Universities.

The coach in Moores was never far away: 'Even as a young player I knew that if possible I wanted to coach full-time. The plan was to play until I was 40 and then coach, hopefully at first-class level. During the winter I was virtually full-time at Hove in the indoor nets in the Gilligan Stand. It was a great experience because one minute you would be coaching a group of 10-year-olds, and the next session might be with a 70-year-old getting his eye in again before the start of the season. There was lots of one-to-one coaching, which I liked, and it gave me a really good grounding.'

Retirement came not at 40 but at 35. He was named player-coach for the 1998 season – also his benefit year – and the captaincy went to Chris Adams, who had signed from Derbyshire. Early in the 1998 season, however, Moores realised that he could not give his best as a coach while he was still a player. He decided to retire in May that year.

'I knew I couldn't do both jobs as well as I wanted to. Fortunately, we'd signed Chris Adams and Michael Bevan, so there was a lot more experience on the field. We just needed someone to organise things off it. I always saw coaching as the next step for me after playing, but it was still a bit of a surprise that it all happened so quickly.'

But just as a back injury almost brought his playing career to an early end in 1986, so his life as a coach nearly came to a premature end. Sussex finished bottom of the Second Division in 2000, and Moores and Adams were almost sacked. Pigott, who was close to both men, would not have done it, but by now he had been succeeded as chief executive by David Gilbert, whom he had brought from Surrey.

It is very difficult to find someone who will bad-mouth Moores. In fact you are required to travel halfway round the globe. Even then the criticism is retrained. But Gilbert says: 'Peter and I clashed. We're both strong-minded characters, and we had our own views about how things should be done. We certainly had our moments.

'No one could ever question Peter's commitment. He was always the first guy on the ground and usually the last to leave. He was very hands-on and dedicated.

'But he doesn't recognise the value of downtime. He gets so absorbed he can be obsessional. Management is all about delegation, and Peter has got to be careful how he balances things.

'I felt that too much power had been vested in the cricket management and that worried me. It looked as if the captain and coach were running the whole club which, in my opinion, was palpably not the right thing.'

Moores also looks back on his relationship with Gilbert with something less than affection. 'There wasn't much laughter between David and myself, and we were never what I'd call mates,' he said.

Pigott said: 'When David Gilbert came down he wanted to bring Keith Medlycott with him. I don't think he and Peter got on particularly well. I had appointed Chris Adams and Peter Moores, but I think David wanted to get his own man in the coaching job.

'If David had stayed I think both Peter and Chris might have gone, but Peter brings an awful lot to cricket, and I think England will benefit hugely in the coming years.'

Fortunately for Moores, Adams and Sussex, Gilbert left to become chief executive of his native New South Wales. Moores and Adams were left in peace to rebuild the club. In 2001 Sussex won the Division Two title. By 2002 Warwickshire were showing an interest in signing the bright young coach; Sussex responded by offering him a fresh four-year contract. Before a ball was bowled that season, Moores was required to show very different qualities. Umer Rashid, the club's gifted all-rounder, was drowned, along with his brother, during a pre-season visit to Grenada. It was left to Moores not only to comfort his devastated players, but also to break the tragic news to the Rashid family.

In 2002 Sussex won only three matches, but they also became the first promoted county not to lose their First Division status the following season. They finished sixth in the table, their best position for 18 years, and steadied themselves for the momentous summer to follow. The winning of the title has been discussed elsewhere in this book. It was the making of the club – and the coach. 'You can't really compare coaching with playing,' he said afterwards. 'In many ways playing is easier – you turn up, perform to the best of your ability and go home. Coaching is all-encompassing, but you get huge satisfaction when it all comes together as it did for us in 2003. It's fun watching people improve. You haven't done it all for them, but you have helped and that gives you a great buzz.'

When he left Sussex in September 2005, Moores said: 'I think one of the nicest things is when people outside recognise what we have achieved and what is now in place here. Yorkshire are one of the biggest counties in the country, so to hear their coach, David Byas, tell me that they see us as a blueprint to follow is enormously satisfying.'

Sussex must have felt flattered all over again when Yorkshire tried to lure their captain, Adams, to Headingley at the end of the 2006 season.

So Moores moved to the Midlands with his wife, Karren, and two children. And just as he went to Lord's in the aftermath of the historic Ashes story of 1981, he took charge of the Academy at a time of great excitement following an even more memorable series against Australia in 2005.

'Our game is buzzing at the moment because of the Ashes success, but what's happening has been coming for four or five years,' he said then. 'Things like central contracts and two divisions have helped increase the intensity levels in our domestic cricket, and with it the skill levels.

'The pool of talent becoming available to England is getting bigger all the time. My predecessor, Rod Marsh, has done a fantastic job and instilled a very strong work ethic, which is something I think I brought to the work I did at Sussex.

'The facilities at Loughborough are the best in the world. Everything is here to help the players improve their games and reach the very top if they want to grab the opportunity.

'As for me, I want it to become a place where excellence is regarded as standard, so that when they get the chance to play at the top level, nothing is going to shock them – they will have been prepared for every challenge which is thrown at them.' This is very similar to something he said when he took over at Hove.

Well, Moores has encountered difficulties since then. Some of the young talent has dried up. But others have developed their games under his guidance, and there was an immediate upturn in the fortunes of the one-day side.

In Moores's place, Mark Robinson has gone on to even greater success. But he never allows anyone to forget that Moores was the man who put everything in place. Bob Paisley was the most successful manager in Liverpool's history – but if you go to their Kop they still talk about the man who built the club up to where it is today, Bill Shankly.

Robinson said: 'The best thing I can say about Peter is that he's a proper person. He is a proper man with proper standards about how people should operate and behave. He stands for everything that's good. And he's a winner. He will never be forgotten here, for what he has done for this club.

'He's got great drive and great vision. And he's determined to establish things that will stay in place after he's gone, whether it's from Sussex or England. He certainly established things at Sussex that have lasted. He's more than just a coach – although he is outstanding at that, too.

'He was a wicketkeeper-batsman, but he just happened to be the best bowling coach I ever had. He puts things across in a way you can understand. Like John Buchanan with Australia, he has proved you can be an outstanding coach without having played the game at international level.

'He has also come into the England job at the right time. A divide has been allowed to grow between the county and the England game, and it's about time county cricket was seen as part of the solution, not part of the problem. Every time something goes wrong it is chucked at county cricket's door. Well, Peter will be able to change that. I think he will help unite the game. He understands the county game very well and knows all the coaches.'

Robinson said he was the best bowling coach he ever had and in New Zealand in 2008 Alastair Cook, the England opening batsman who had endured a torrid time in the field in Sri Lanka, took some blinding catches and said Moores was the finest fielding coach he had ever had.

Chris Adams, meanwhile, perhaps his greatest ally in his days at Hove, is convinced that good times are ahead for England. 'I believe English cricket is ready for someone to take it to the next level and that Peter is that man. He's a very different person to Duncan Fletcher and has a different style. He's very hands on, is a terrific one-on-one coach and he sees his main role as making his players excited to play cricket every day.

'One player has said that he has this magic dust which he throws around and which makes players perform. He creates an environment in which players are happy to perform. I think he will be a revelation with England.'

It all started for Moores at Sussex. And it all started for Sussex with Moores.

Chapter 10
Into an Uncertain Future

MARK ROBINSON'S biggest fear, when he starts talking about Sussex's future, is not the impending retirement of his inspirational captain and his leg-spinner. It is money.

The gap between the haves and have-nots in English football started to widen as soon as the top clubs formed the Premier League in 1994, and millions of pounds from TV revenue and sponsorship started to swill around the game.

Of course, there will never be a day when even a regular England cricketer has the earning power of a jobbing Premier League footballer, even if, as seems likely, our top players will soon be supplementing their income with stints in the lucrative new Indian Premier League competition. But like the have-nots in English football, it is becoming increasingly difficult for smaller counties – and despite their phenomenal success of the last five years, that is what Sussex are and will remain – to compete for even average home-grown players, particularly when they are up against clubs whose income is enhanced by staging international cricket.

As an example, the £390,000 loss Sussex made in 2006 would be comfortably swallowed up by the profit Lancashire made from car parking and catering alone in the same period. And that's not from cricket matches, but from the use of their facilities by Manchester United supporters on match days at the other Old Trafford. Sussex's membership is just 4,000 – one of the smallest in the country – and while the success of Twenty20 cricket has shown that there is an appetite in the county for cricket in the bite-sized chunks offered by the shortest format of the game it is difficult to underestimate how parlous their finances would be were it not for the £12 million left to them by Spen Cama when he died in June 2001, aged 92.

That windfall from their former president not only ensured the immediate future of the club, it also enabled them to start planning for a future when cricket will represent only a modest part of the club's overall income. There were some immediate spin-offs from the legacy. In 2003 a new indoor school and changing-room complex, named after the benefactor who funded it, was opened with money borrowed against Cama's legacy. But the redevelopment of the County Ground, which has been on the cards since 2004, is taking a painfully long time to materialise.

Although £400,000 was spent upgrading the pavilion to bring it into line with the requirements of the Safety of Sports Grounds Act, the grand vision of David Green, who has just started his seventh year as chairman, and his committee was a development at the Sea End of the ground. Initially, this would involve demolishing the Gilligan Stand. The 100 or so seats on top provide the best viewing area in the ground, but the wrecking ball cannot come quickly enough for one of the biggest eyesores on the county circuit. On a sunny afternoon, if you are reclining in a deckchair at the Cromwell Road end, it is hard to believe the two areas are part of the same ground as you cast your eye towards the sea. In its place will eventually rise a new public pavilion, finally offering shelter and decent matchday facilities for non-members. There will be improved spectator seating in a wide sweep all the way along the southern end of the ground, with new hospitality boxes, improved facilities for the corporate market and a conference facility, all designed to bring in revenue all the year round rather than just when cricket is being played. Not only that, but Sussex have also planned an even more ambitious development for the site of the Sussex Cricketer pub at the entrance to the ground in Eaton Road. This would incorporate a hotel and luxury flats, with office accommodation to help offset the cost. But four years after these plans were first aired publicly, the builders have not moved in.

When the property and financial markets worldwide started to experience a downturn in the summer of 2007, Green could see the signs. He called a halt to the second part of the development because of the increasingly uncertain economic situation, preferring instead to channel all of his energies into finally getting work underway at the sea end.

But nothing at Sussex is ever easy, or so it seems. This is the club, remember, which in the mid-1990s talked ambitiously about developing the Cromwell Road end of the ground. Members, many of whom

Full house. Twenty20 cricket continues to attract big crowds to the County Ground. And those are extra seats.

would have lost their favourite vantage point from the blue-and-white-striped deckchairs, were sceptical, and they had every reason to be. It turned out that Sussex could barely afford the architect's drawings, and the idea was quietly shelved.

Green's biggest achievement so far has been overseeing the building of the new indoor school in 2004. It is a facility much admired by other counties and provides a proper environment for the development of the next generation of Sussex cricketers. Increasingly, it seems, counties like Sussex will have to build their teams around players they have developed themselves, and in that regard Sussex are in good shape. Their Academy system and youth-development programme is one of the best in the country, and it must be a source of satisfaction to Mark Robinson and his coaching staff that of the 21 players who were charged with trying to bring a third successive Championship to the club in 2008, 13 learned their cricket with the county.

It is a trend which is likely to continue. As well as struggling to compete financially for English players, Sussex may find the market for overseas talent diminishing. What self-respecting international cricketer will want to slog his way around England for five months when he can earn two or three times as much for six weeks' work in the new cash-rich Indian Premier League? While Kolpak-qualified players continue to flood the market, with more soon to become available when New Zealand and Australia conclude a 'trade' agreement with the United Kingdom, Sussex have been reluctant to follow the likes of Northamptonshire and Leicestershire in recruiting heavily from that source.

When Murray Goodwin became Kolpak 'qualified' in 2004, the county insisted that he would be the first and the last player recruited that way. But needs must, and when the ECB cut the number of overseas players counties were able to employ down to one for the 2008 season they began a protracted search for a replacement for Rana Naved. Ryan Harris was signed only to disappear after playing just one game, when he joined Queensland Bulls.

Replenishing their fast-bowling stocks this way is not Sussex's preferred *modus operandi*. But there is a desperate lack of young fast-bowling talent in the county and has been for years. Youngsters these days want to be batsmen, all-rounders or leg-spinners. Robinson's long-term objective is clear. He will not risk the county's financial stability in the quest for more trophies.

'Our supporters have to understand that they don't support a big club,' he said. 'We simply cannot compete with the huge salaries some counties can offer if they want to sign a player.

'There is one small pot of money at a club like ours, and the amount in that pot hasn't really changed, despite the success over the past five years. It goes up but it needs to simply for us to stand still.'

Robinson offers an example of how every penny counts. There is no doubting the prestige of playing for the last two years in the annual curtain-raiser to the new season against MCC at Lord's. A competitive run-out ahead of the serious stuff, it is a fixture not without merit. Robinson agrees, while reconciling himself to the fact that his budget will be several thousand pounds lighter because he has to pay for four nights' hotel accommodation and associated costs for what is, essentially, a friendly.

His job is always to look one step ahead. When his big players come out of contract, there is little he can do if another county makes a bid for their services with a better financial offer. 'That's being realistic, not pessimistic,' he said.

'What we can offer, which other clubs can't, is the best support a player could get anywhere in the world. We offer them a better way of life than anywhere else – and we're winners.

'We want the likes of Adams, Mushtaq and Prior to play for Sussex as long as they can. What I can't do is bankrupt the club – everyone has their price. Big players come and go at every club, but life goes on. The aim here has and always will be to keep the side together as long as possible.

'It is a juggling act, but my job is no different to a manager of a small football club. You have to make tough decisions sometimes, but you are always looking to the future.

'People also have to understand that we have to reward existing players who have done well, such as Mike Yardy and Luke Wright, because they are the sort of players we want to build the club's long-term future around.'

Robinson's cause is undoubtedly helped by the generosity of Sussex's sponsors. The Players Club was formed in 2004 by Peter Moores as an exclusive association for 20 members whose fees go straight into the professional cricket budget. The signings of Goodwin and, in 2007, Saqlain Mushtaq, were only possible thanks to the Players Club, while their financial input also enabled the county to employ a full-time strength-and-conditioning coach.

One of the founder members is Clive Roberts, who has business interests in travel and wine, and who owns the Old Forge restaurant in Storrington, a frequent haunt of Sussex players, particularly during Arundel week.

'I think the Players Club contributes to the most important thing in a cricket club: having good players and winning,' Roberts said. 'We contribute funds that specifically go into Mark Robinson's budget rather than into the general club pot. Rather than relying on the money, he talks to us about his specific needs. In my opinion, if he didn't have a good reason we wouldn't pay the money.'

Ian Cameron, who runs a successful direct-mailing business, is another founder member. 'The money from the Players Club has directly helped us win three Championships in five years,' he says. 'We are the only county to have such a club, which is partly because we have so many sponsors at Sussex but also because the players know the sponsors here.'

In return, the sponsors are invited to player-only social events. Many were on the balcony when the Championship successes of 2006 and 2007 were being boisterously celebrated. 'It is nice to know that in the dressing room there is a list of Players Club members so the players know who is involved,' said Roberts.

The difficult job of overseeing Sussex's finances on a day-to-day basis is in the hands of chief executive Gus Mackay, who joined the county from Leicestershire in September 2006, and treasurer Jim May, one of the disillusioned members who helped get rid of the discredited management set-up in 1997.

'Success brings high costs in terms of salaries and bonuses, but there is expectation at the club now,' says Mackay. 'We increased the cricket budget by 10 per cent for 2008, and it is up to the club to generate more revenue so we can stay successful. We have 3,500 members, which is six per cent up, but I would like us to have 4,000 with more juniors.'

There is no doubt that the introduction of the Twenty20 Cup has offered clubs such as Sussex a financial lifeline. In 2008 the competition has been expanded for the second time to guarantee five home matches for each county. Three of Sussex's four games last season were 7,000 sell-outs, and there is a greater incentive for teams to reach the Finals this year, with both Finalists going on to compete in the inaugural World Twenty20 Championship in India, where the prize for the winners is a staggering £1 million. With Twenty20 taking off in India, the profile of the domestic competition is sure to continue to increase. The day when counties sign overseas stars specifically for the competition are not far away.

Cricket has been played at the County Ground in Hove 'between Mr Ridgen's farm and the station at Cliftonville' since 1872. The first pavilion was erected at a cost of less than £700, membership was two guineas and a roller-skating rink was built where the Gilligan Stand is set (for a few more months at least). You wonder what the spectators who saw Lillywhite and Southern take 84 of the 113 wickets that fell in the six first-class matches of that inaugural season would make of Twenty20 cricket, coloured clothing and the other paraphernalia of the modern game.

Fortunately, those charged with ushering the club towards an uncertain future are as proud and respectful of the traditions of Sussex cricket as their forefathers. 'I will fight anyone who tries to take away the things which make us a special club,' said Robinson. 'Our togetherness.'

Cameron, a big Sussex man in every sense, added: 'You are writing this book too soon – we're going to win the Championship again in 2008.'

Index

ND - #0366 - 270225 - C0 - 260/195/12 - PB - 9781780914275 - Gloss Lamination